hands across the caviar

by the author of BEARS IN THE CAVIAR

Charles

hands across

V. Thayer

the caviar

J. B. Lippincott Company
Philadelphia & New York

copyright, 1952, by Charles W. Thayer

first edition

*printed in the United States of America
by H. Wolff, New York
designed by Marshall Lee*

Library of Congress Catalog Card Number 52–10934

contents

hands across the caviar

*drink doesn't affect me; or
how to get along with
the Russians*

according

to someone, who ought to know, the most fatal of famous last words are "Drink-doesn't-affect-me" and "I-can-get-along-with-the-Russians."

For seven long years, as a secretary at our Moscow Embassy, I'd tried to explode the theory. But after every attempt, whether it was a cocktail party or a masked ball, I'd ended up with a headache and a taciturn "nyet" from the Soviet officials I'd tried to make friends with. But perhaps, I thought, this was the fault of the Moscow atmosphere with its microphones, GPU agents and spies. Get a Russian outside, in a Paris sidewalk cafe for instance, and he would be different. Then he couldn't dismiss with a quotation from *Pravda* the realities that bustled past before his eyes. He couldn't tell you that the sleek workmen walking by were starving. He couldn't tell you that the preposterous fellow in the corner reading the Communist *Humanité* was a blindfolded victim of capitalism. He'd have to abandon his distorted vocabulary and start talking in terms of reality instead of *Pravda's* make-believe. Then, I thought, you could begin to find a basis of understanding and, eventually, confidence, if not friendship.

The world, when I left Russia for the last time in 1942, was not perhaps the best place to prove my contention. But even despite the war there was occasionally some beauty and above all there was the power of the allied armies to refute the Bolshevik picture of decadent capitalism. So I still believed you could make a Soviet official trust you and talk sense if you just got him outside the zoo Stalin had built for him.

My first try was in Afghanistan. Kabul perhaps wasn't quite as promising as Paris, but by then Paris was in the hands of Hitler, Stalin's erstwhile partner; and at least Kabul could boast of itself as an independent, fairly prosperous country where the peasants and tribesmen were no less well off than the collective farmers of Russia, despite the absence of Stalin and communism. So when the young Counselor of the Soviet Embassy came around for dinner, I put my theory to the test. Very gingerly I suggested that the world wasn't all black and white, Soviet good and non-Soviet bad, capitalist rot and Stalinist vitality. When the Counselor left I thought I'd made a good beginning.

But the next day his boss, the Russian Ambassador, asked me to lunch with him alone.

"My Counselor tells me," he began as soon as we'd sat down, "that you find certain things about Russia not entirely satisfactory."

I nodded.

"He said that you believe, for instance, that despite collectivization the Russian peasant doesn't eat better than the Afghan. In fact, if he reported the conversation correctly, you thought there was a certain shortage of food in 1933 and again in 1940 just before the Hitler attack."

I nodded again.

"I appreciate how difficult it must be for a foreigner to understand everything in Russia. But to say that there was a famine in 1933 or hunger in 1940 is utter nonsense."

"But I saw it myself," I protested. "I was in the villages in 1933 and again in 1940. I saw the peasants eating the crows they'd asked me to shoot for them. Surely a well-fed peasant doesn't prefer crows."

"As a Russian who has also visited the villages, I must insist that there was no lack of food in the Russian countryside in 1940 or at any other time since the Revolution."

"But—" I began again.

"What is more," the Ambassador went on, "I hope in the interests of friendship between our two countries that you will not express to the Afghans the views you gave my Counselor. After all, we are allies and, as a West Pointer, you should appreciate the difficulties of our military position. Under these conditions we must not let the Afghans get the impression there are any flaws in our political system."

I wondered whether he applied the same rules in his discussions with Afghans on the American system.

Later I was sent as a secretary to the European Advisory Commission in London where the Russians, the British and ourselves were trying to plan the future of post-war Europe. My Russian opposite member was a humorous bright young fellow who'd been a chemical engineer till he was suddenly mobilized for the Diplomatic Service. At the very first meeting of the Commission's Secretariat he had produced an English dictionary of American slang "to avoid any misunderstandings between my British and American colleagues," he explained solemnly.

When the Secretary General suggested the following Tuesday for the next meeting, he quickly consulted his pocket calendar and commented, "Well, it doesn't make much difference to an atheist like myself but have you Christians considered that next Tuesday is the second Tuesday after Epiphany, whatever that is?"

On the whole he looked like more promising material than the Soviet Counselor in Kabul and I cultivated him carefully. He reciprocated by inviting me out to dinner at the Royal Automobile Club. The way he rolled out the "Royal" you'd never have suspected his Government had exterminated Russia's royalty only twenty-five years before. When I stopped at his office in Lancaster House to pick him up on the way to dinner, he produced a full bottle of Bourbon from his desk drawer, explaining, "I've ordered a table at the Club in half an hour, so we'd better be quick about it if we're going to finish this." By the time we rolled unsteadily into the Automobile Club I wasn't in the best shape to start a serious discussion of basic realities. But I made a try at it.

"Do you think," I asked, "that in spite of the obvious dangers, there might be some advantages to Russia in letting Germany keep a certain amount of industrial capacity after the war?"

He looked at me coldly across the dreary English wartime cooking. "Listen, I've come out to enjoy myself, not to get dialectic. Besides I'm just a simple chemical engineer who doesn't understand such problems." Then he signalled the waiter for another bottle of wine.

The next day when my boss, George Kennan, asked me if my Soviet friend had given any clues on Russia's post-war plans, I had to admit, "Nothing that I can remember except that he can drink like a fish. You don't by chance happen to have an aspirin handy?"

But I still wasn't convinced. A month or two later as the

negotiations in the EAC dragged on fruitlessly, I met an old friend, Fitzroy MacLean, at Claridge's Bar. Fitzroy and I had been junior secretaries together in Moscow five years before. Since then he'd managed to get out of the British diplomatic service by standing for election to Parliament. (I've often wondered whether there's anything significant in the fact that in America you run for election whereas in England you simply stand.) Somewhat to his dismay, Fitzroy not only stood but he got elected while he was still in the rear rank learning close order drill. But the British Army soon straightened that out and made him a captain and later a brigadier. After a couple of years spent in abducting obstreperous German agents in the Middle East and disrupting Rommel's African supply lines, he was chosen by Prime Minister Churchill in 1943 to parachute into Yugoslavia and head up an Anglo-American Military Mission to Tito.

Fitzroy told me that the Anglo-American Mission was now being split into two and that General Donovan of the OSS was organizing a separate American Mission. Why not see if Donovan wouldn't send me as the political member of the U. S. Mission? Fitzroy asked.

"It's very interesting," he insisted, "and think of all the Russians you'll see when the Red Army gets there!"

I was reminded of the dozens of Allied Military Attachés and observers sitting idly in Moscow waiting for a chance to visit the Russian front. With the exception of a few carefully conducted tours of quiet sectors no one had ever seen the Red Army at all.

If we were attached to the Yugoslav Partisans we'd have an opportunity, probably the only opportunity for western observers, unguarded, unguided and free to see what we chose, to observe a Russian army in action. It was not a chance to miss.

"i wouldn't

smoke in the plane if I were you," the Captain warned us. "Those sacks are full of dynamite."

I thought I'd misunderstood and asked him to repeat.

"Yes," he shouted again over the roar of the engines, "that's high explosive for Brother Tito. If you're able to land you can give it to him yourself. If you have to jump, tell him we'll send it as soon as he gets a landing strip working."

With our parachutes strapped to our backs, we clambered up the ladder and through the doorless opening into the plane.

"Don't we even have a door on this crate?" I asked a little sourly. "It gets cold up there sometimes."

"Hell! You don't need a door," the Captain shouted. "It got ripped off a couple of days back. The fresh air will do you good. Besides it's easier to get out if you have to jump. And don't forget—"

"to-count-ten-before-you-pull-the-cord," I anticipated him wearily. "Yes, I know."

"No! Don't forget that's high explosive," he called, pointing to the sacks that filled the fuselage up to the windows. "It makes fairly comfortable bedding, but it's no good for camp fires." With this final flash of wit he signalled the pilot to get going.

It was well after dark and we could hardly see the metal runway as we taxied back and forth interminably over the bumpy South Italian airfield. But at last the pilot put his foot on the accelerator, or whatever pilots do to gain speed, and we started down the runway in a deafening lunge. The tail came up and we bounced a time or two on the landing wheels. Suddenly the engine died. We settled back on the tail and the wheel brakes screeched angrily as we slowly lost speed and stopped.

The co-pilot stuck his head out of the pilot's cabin and explained that one of the dozens of indicators on the dashboard wasn't indicating. It would only take a minute to fix it and then we'd be off.

Eventually we got off the ground, TNT and all, and were skimming low over the Adriatic headed for Serbia where the Partisans had promised they'd have a landing strip ready for us. My companion was Lieutenant Bill Callanan, a fellow member of the newly organized American Mission to Yugoslavia, or as General Donovan insisted on calling it, "The Independent U.S. Military Mission to Marshal Tito." The word "Independent" was to call attention to the fact that it was no longer part of the Anglo-American Military Mission.

The head of the American Mission was Colonel Ellery Huntington.

Huntington had played quarterback for Yale back around the turn of the century. Ever since, whenever he got a chance to call signals, he would carry the ball himself right through center in spite of the fact that he was hardly five feet tall. Keeping fit was Huntington's hobby and he managed to keep his muscles at about the consistency of a nail. But however seriously he might take his muscles or his chest measurements, he fortunately never took himself too seriously. He was one of that rare species of chicken colonels who could take a joke on himself with a grin and come back for more.

Huntington had picked as his deputy Major Stafford Reid, a fellow New Yorker. Reid to his disappointment had been left in charge of the Mission's headquarters on the summer resort Island of Vis in the Adriatic. He, like Huntington, preferred battlefields to bathing beaches.

When we took off for Serbia, Colonel Huntington and the radio operator, Sergeant Muselin, were in another C-47 ahead of us. In a third plane was MacLean. Our immediate mission, as I understood it, was to find Tito who had recently taken a powder from his headquarters on the Island of Vis. Exactly what we were supposed to do when we found him wasn't very clear.

When Germany invaded Yugoslavia in 1941 and smashed her small army, two guerrilla leaders took to the hills and started to wage war on the Axis. One was Mikhailovitch, a Royalist. The other was Tito, a Communist. Neither was very fond of the other and both of them asked the Allies for exclusive assistance. Faced with this dilemma the world at large promptly and vehemently took sides, seizing a torch either for Mikhailovitch's Chetniks or for Tito's Partisans.

There were plenty of arguments to supply both sides with

oratory and literature for years, and no lack of that hysterical emotionalism Yugoslavia seems to generate in her admirers whenever trouble brews in the Balkans.

Originally Mikhailovitch, who was the first in the field, or rather in the forests, fighting the Germans, was generally accepted as the legitimate leader. But after Germany attacked Russia, Tito, the Communist, took to the woods and began collecting followers at a great rate. In the early days Tito and Mikhailovitch tried to work together against the Germans. But cooperation was not their long suit and soon ugly rumors from both sides began coming out of the Balkans. Tito, Mikhailovitch reported, was a mere tool of Stalin bent on conquering Yugoslavia for the Soviet Union. Consequently, Mikhailovitch alleged, Tito was murdering Chetniks and leaving the Germans alone. Whereupon Tito retorted that Mikhailovitch was attacking his Partisans and collaborating with the Italians and Germans.

As early as 1942, the U.S. and Britain started sending missions into the woods of Croatia and Serbia to get the facts. But the reports of these missions were conflicting and confusing. If you went to Mikhailovitch you got one story. If you went to Tito you got an opposite story. If you went to both you got neither, for each side would consider you a spy. In those early days of the war such missions were no easy undertakings. In the first place you had to contrive to drop into the country without landing in enemy hands. Then you had to find the faction you were sent to. Then you had to hide with them, tramp up and down the mountains through snow and storms with them; often, for self protection, you had to fight with them, and finally, get out. A parachute has one distinct disadvantage: it travels in only one direction. When the parachutist wants to go back up again he's not going to get much help from his 'chute. Many an investigator got in, investigated and radioed back his report in short order, but when he himself tried to get out found himself caught in a trap.

Among the Americans who took part in those early missions was Captain "Slim" Farish, later killed in an aircrash in Greece. Colonel Weil, who was to be President of Macy's, was another early bird in the field and was one of the few who got to both the Chetniks and the Partisans. Colonel Mc-Dowell, a well-known Balkan expert, had been sent to Mikhailovitch and was still with him when I first arrived in the autumn of 1944.

McDowell's presence in Mikhailovitch's camp used to burn up the Partisans who by now claimed to be the only legitimate Allies in the woods. A year before, in 1943, Churchill had decided that Tito was killing the most Germans. So Tito had been getting the lion's share of Allied help. Since Roosevelt and Churchill had agreed the Balkans were primarily a British responsibility, as the Pacific was ours, we had acquiesced in the decision. But we still wanted to keep an eye on the Chetniks. Our curiosity seemed reasonable enough to me, but to Tito it was plain "treachery." I often wondered what word he'd have used if he'd found out that Stalin had also wanted to send a mission to Mikhailovitch a year earlier.

Stalin had been a good deal more cautious than Churchill when it came to choosing sides in the Balkans. He naturally wanted his Communists to get ahead in the world, but at the same time he desperately needed an active guerrilla war in the Balkans to draw off German divisions from his own fronts. From bitter experiences in Germany, Czechoslovakia, Hungary, and Rumania, he had found his Communist Parties rather less than brilliant in stirring up civil wars. So Stalin waited a whole year, till 1944, before he finally put his chips openly on Tito and sent in a mission under an elderly ex-Czarist officer, Lieutenant General Korneev, a highly educated old gentleman with a thinly veiled contempt for his uncouth

Slav brethren of the Balkans. Korneev was, however, a sick man and most of the time I was in Yugoslavia the Soviet Mission was commanded by his deputy, Major General Kisiliev.

By the autumn of 1944 most of the bugs had been ironed out of the Balkan transportation and supply service. Submissions of Americans and British were operating throughout the country from northern Carinthia and Austria right down to Macedonia and Greece in the south. The main purpose of the sub-missions was to tell AFHQ in Caserta what the guerrillas needed most in the way of supplies and then arrange nocturnal parachute drops. They also improvised landing strips from which the guerrilla wounded could be evacuated to Army Hospitals in Italy or Egypt. As a sideline they frequently organized little dynamiting parties to blow up bridges, tunnels and other items of value to Hitler. So it was relatively simple by the time I arrived to get into Yugoslavia and almost as simple, God and the Air Force willing, to get out again.

Politically, too, the task was comparatively simplified by the fact that minds had already been made up and the big question was not whom to help but what the consequences were going to be. In answering that question many of us, including myself, turned out to be wrong for what I still think were the very best reasons. Others turned out to be right for what I'm sure were precisely the wrong reasons. But that's not part of this story.

Such was the situation as I had gathered it from innumerable briefings and endless discussions in the State Department, in the Pentagon, and in the officers' clubs of Caserta and Bari. Here again the emotional qualities of Yugoslav politics had been contagious. Scarcely an officer who had anything to do with the Chetniks or Partisans had not taken sides violently.

At the Silver Foxhole, OSS Headquarters in Caserta, even the Post Surgeon, a calm and otherwise highly reasonable officer, had turned on me as I sat down to my first breakfast.

"So you're jumping into the Partisans, I hear?" and before I could reply he added almost snarling, "You'll soon find out you're on the wrong side."

I thought the Colonel was a little unreasonable. In the first place, I don't believe in talk of any kind at breakfast. Secondly, if I have a parachute jump ahead of me, as I thought I did, I don't think it's fair to refer to it on an empty stomach. And finally, I didn't like the implication that I'd voted Communist at the last Yugoslav General Election. Talleyrand once advised an aspiring young diplomat, *"Surtout pas trop de zèle."* "Keep your shirt on" sounded like a pretty good rule that night when we headed out for Serbia.

We were skimming low over the water. There was no moon. Moons are unpopular with parachutists. But the stars were out and you could see the slightly rippling waters of the Adriatic only forty or fifty feet below us.

A red light flashed on beside us and Bill Callanan, an old hand in these flights, explained it was a warning that we were approaching the Dalmatian Coast, probably near Dubrovnik and within range of German anti-aircraft fire. Just before taking off, we'd been told an earlier flight to Rumania had reported heavy German flak along the Coast. The engines were beginning to breathe a little harder and I could feel the plane climbing. A few minutes later there was a rush of wind and a cloud of white flakes fluttered in the open door covering us in a bed of what looked like snow.

"Now what the hell?"

"They're just propaganda leaflets," Bill explained calmly. "I guess the pilot dropped them out the window up front and the backwash blew them back in." He began to gather them up and toss them back out the open doorway. "OWI claims that there are some Dalmatian peasants who can read," he added.

"Who writes them?" I asked.

"OWI," Bill answered, "and I hate to think what they say." As a matter of standard wartime Government practice, OWI and OSS didn't exactly see eye-to-eye on the Yugoslav problem. At the moment OWI was rooting for the Chetniks and Bill was a staunch Partisan. But he threw the leaflets out anyway, apparently confident that the Dalmatians couldn't read.

For a couple more hours we droned on over Montenegro and Bosnia. Once an anti-aircraft searchlight flashed on and began to sweep the sky ominously. But it didn't pick up our planes and soon went out. If any German flak was around, it wasn't interested in us. Eventually we felt the plane coming down and banking into a turn. For several minutes we circled hesitantly above a black and inhospitable countryside. Then the pilot spotted the "pinpoint," a tiny bonfire somewhere below us. We circled some more to throw off any enemy observers who might be searching for our secret landing strip. Then we closed in cautiously at tree-top height till we could see the row of kerosene-filled tin cans indicating the runway. The flaps went down and we slowed to a mere hundred miles an hour. A moment later, the wheels touched, bounced back into the air, touched again, and we coasted bumpily to a halt.

The engines were throttled back but were kept turning over. A crowd of curious faces peered through the doorway. Eager hands began to grab the sacks of high explosive. In a few minutes the plane was unloaded and was taxiing gingerly back to the end of the runway.

Huntington, MacLean and the rest of us were bundled into a truck. As we drove off, we could just see the C-47 take off again into the moonless night. It gave you a rather eerie sensation to see your only link with civilization disappearing, a dim shadow among the stars.

MacLean turned to his Liaison Officer, Major Freddy Cole, who'd met us.

"Where's Tito?"

"Don't know."

Freddy was a tough young officer who'd spent most of his adult life fighting in the Western Desert or with Tito's Partisans. Though not exactly the Guards Officer type, he knew how to take care of himself, do his job and enjoy himself thoroughly on and off duty.

"Where's Arso?" MacLean asked.

"He arrived last night from Vis with a half dozen officers of the Supreme Staff and the Russian Military Mission."

"Where's Peko?"

"He's here all right. Planning to move on Belgrade soon."

Tito, Arso, Peko, the nicknames of leading Partisans, sounded strangely informal after the "General This" and "Field Marshal That" we were used to back in AFHQ in Italy. It wasn't till we got to Belgrade that Tito began to make his title of "Marshal" stick. Arso, his Chief of Staff, then became General Jovanovic. Peko, the Commander of the Partisan elite First Corps, became General Dapcevic.

For an hour we bounced about on the floor of the truck as we raced without headlights along what had once been a cobblestone highway. I was dying to ask some questions myself but as a newcomer I was afraid to show my dumbness. But at last I screwed up my courage and asked Cole where we were and where we were heading. It sounded like a reasonable enough question, but Freddy, who'd been chasing about the countryside on foot for months, evidently found it pretty amateurish.

"We're in the Shumadija headed for Valjevo," he snapped, indicating that that was sufficient information for anyone who had any sense at all. This left me approximately where I was when I broached the matter but I took the hint and asked no more silly questions.

Eventually the truck reached a blacked-out, deserted town. "Valjevo," Freddy announced like a tourist guide. "We captured it from the Heinies a fortnight ago. It was a hell of a fight—good show!" Freddy had been serving a long time with First Corps and not unjustifiably considered himself one of the gang. I felt more like a neophyte than ever.

We stopped in front of a suburban villa which Freddy said had been assigned to the Americans. There were no lights but with the help of a flashlight we managed to find some beds and unroll our sleeping bags. The owner, our landlady, appeared with a bottle of cherry brandy to welcome us and we each took a polite swig or two. Her husband, she explained briefly, had been shot by the Germans in reprisal for a guerrilla raid. He'd been one of the leading merchants in the town and she was a bit concerned about the attitude the Communist Partisans might take to such bourgeois elements. So she was more than delighted to welcome some Capitalist Americans into her home, though for the life of her she couldn't figure out why Americans were wandering about this part of the world at this stage of affairs. But as it was already three a.m., we didn't try to explain our presence. Instead we turned in quickly and were soon asleep for our first night "in the woods," as we subsequently referred to it with deep pride and shameless inaccuracy.

Valjevo, I found out next day, is a small farming town of seventeen thousand inhabitants ninety-five kilometers southwest of Belgrade. When we arrived the citizens were still a little stunned by the arrival of the Partisans who, they'd been led to believe, were a highly questionable species of marauder.

Freddy Cole described with great relish and pride how

the First Corps had managed to chase off the relatively strong
German garrison quartered in the fortified military barracks
on a hill overlooking the town. First, over a period of nights
the Partisans had stealthily surrounded the town on all sides.
Then they brought up several pieces of mountain artillery,
an innovation in their military equipment which they'd got
from AFHQ just a few days before. They'd even managed to
arrange for some light bombers from Italy to shoot up the
fortress with rockets. Surprised by the double novelty of Partisan artillery and rockets the Germans had pulled out after
a short but hot fight. Quick success was essential to Partisan
fighting since the Germans could in the long run always rein-
force an isolated garrison by mechanized columns which
the guerrillas couldn't stop. In fact when the Germans evacuated Valjevo, a relief column was already on the way but
turned back when it met the retreating German garrison.

In the town there had been relatively little fighting. The
scars of a few bursts of light machine gun fire at street corners, a few windows smashed by grenades, two or three
houses burned out, were the only signs of war. The house into
which "The Independent American Military Mission" moved
had been the headquarters of the former German Town
Commandant. He'd been taken completely by surprise and
both he and his adjutant were killed before they could reach
the street. A patch of bullet holes in the walls of the living
room indicated the action had been lively.

What struck me most about Valjevo was the great number
of men, young and old, who lolled about in the shady streets
and listlessly watched the Partisan soldiers coming and going, hauling food and fodder, cleaning equipment, drilling
and marching. If Valjevo was typical, the great majority of
manpower in Serbia stood aside with sullen hostility while a
small minority fought their way to power over the hard-
pressed Germans. Only after the capture of Belgrade did

Tito turn his attention to mobilizing these "neutral" elements into the Partisan Army or into labor battalions. Later, during the process of this mobilization, when a Partisan newspaper announced that poor Serbs enlisting in the Army would be eligible for free funerals, one cynic remarked that there was good reason to believe that those who didn't enlist would be granted the same privilege.

From the Partisan leaders we also got a description of the local military situation. The Germans, they said, were headed north toward Belgrade through which lay the chief escape route for their remaining divisions retreating north from Greece and west from the Rumanian and Bulgarian frontiers which Tolbukhin's Third Ukrainian Front (Army Group) had already passed. Belgrade and the line of retreat running northwest to Zagreb were vital to the Germans if any of the four to five German divisions still in the south were to get out alive. The Russians, however, had crossed the Danube at the Iron Gates and were striking due west to cut the Belgrade-Athens Highway. The Partisans hoped to make contact with them in a few days of marching eastward. Once they'd established contact, they planned to turn north toward Belgrade.

To the Partisans, Belgrade meant victory. Perhaps not the end of the war with Germany, for that was an assignment Eisenhower and Zhukov were carrying out at the frontiers of Germany itself. But once in their capital on the Danube Tito and his followers knew that Mikhailovitch was finished. From then on power was theirs though it might take a little consolidating and necessitate some "cleaning up" of undesirable elements. However, that was a technical police job..

As soon as we'd settled down in Valjevo, I read the latest reports from the American and British sub-missions in the field. A couple of Allied officers had come up from Macedonia and we talked for hours about Partisan and Chetnik politics on the Greek frontier. In a jumble of Russian and newly acquired Serbian I chatted with the local townspeople and farmers. With the aid of a Serbo-Croat dictionary I struggled through the pages of the local paper. The stories I got were all pretty much the same.

Then I sat down under an apple tree in the garden of our villa and wrote my first political report. Its tune was one I was going to sing hundreds of times in my reports of the next eight months. Tito, the Communist, I wrote, was here to stay. Whether we liked it or not we'd better get used to it unless we were prepared to take on the Red Army along with the Wehrmacht.

Then Sergeant Muselin got busy scrambling about the trees stringing an aerial for his radio set while Bill Callanan and I laboriously coded the message. Bill hated coding even more than I did and frequently he'd ask why I couldn't be a little less wordy. Pompously I told him State Department style was not to be tampered with. Then Bill, too, got busy on his specialty Battle Order. He talked to the Partisan G-2 and the Russian Mission giving them what dope we had on the German Divisions facing Eisenhower and Alexander and getting in return such meagre information as the Russians and Partisans had on the enemy forces facing them. It wasn't too much, but at least when we'd telegraphed it to AFHQ and SHAEF they knew they needn't worry about the whereabouts of the Prince Eugen Division or the First Mountain Division which was presently pinned down by the Reds and the Partisans around Belgrade.

With our first jobs done we settled down to the problem of living. The day after our arrival Tito's Chief of Staff, Arso, who was in command in Valjevo invited us to lunch at his mess in a requisitioned restaurant. The Shumadija District is one of the richest agricultural parts of Serbia. Since the Partisans had been keeping the railroads and roads leading out of the area in a perpetual state of disruption, the Germans had been unable to ship out the Shumadija's grain, eggs, milk, meat, cheese and wines. So in spite of an influx of refugees from Belgrade there was plenty of food for everybody.

After months of the super-austerity of English cooking, that first meal in Serbia was a milestone. The first course was an egg shirred in a sauce of Trappist cheese. Then came a breaded veal steak fried in butter with stuffed Serbian peppers. Next came some moussaka, a casserole dish made of egg, potatoes and lamb with a cream sauce. When we'd eaten what we thought was our fill the waiters marched in again, trays held high over their heads, each with a whole suckling pig. When finally an enormous cake buried in fresh fruits and whipped cream came in, I gave up. If this was guerrilla life behind enemy lines, I decided I was going to change my profession. MacLean, Cole and our Partisan companions, however, hastened to explain that nothing like this had ever happened before. Until now life had been at best combat rations and frostbites.

Back at our quarters we were still licking our chops when word came from Arso that from now on it would be best if the British and Americans established their own mess. Partisan Headquarters Commissary would be glad to supply us with essentials. Evidently the proximity of the Russian armies was already having its effect on Arso. From now on he wouldn't have to be polite to the Westerners. We sighed, shrugged our shoulders and asked Freddy Cole to start organizing a mess. "And it had better be as good as Arso's," we warned him.

Freddy's big problem was a chef. They don't grow on trees even in the Shumadija, but by dinner time, a meal every bit as good as Arso's was served up. We asked Freddy how he'd done it. Where had he found a second chef?

"I didn't," Freddy grinned slyly. "I took Arso's."

"Just how do you go about stealing chefs from the Partisan Chief of Staff?" I asked.

"Easy," Freddy said. "I just did a spot of investigating. Discovered his chef used to work for Prince Paul, the Regent. So I told the Headquarters' Mess Chief about it and asked him how Tito would like it if he knew he had a collaborationist for a cook. So he fired the chef and I hired him. Simple," Freddy concluded and grinned again.

Stepan, the chef, stayed with us as long as I was in Yugoslavia. One evening several months later, after Tito had dined with me he complimented me on the dinner. I smiled deprecatingly and acted as though I'd cooked the meal myself. But Tito wasn't fooled and the next day his secretary, Olga, called and said the Marshal would very much appreciate it if the Colonel (meaning me) would give him his cook. Just in time I remembered Freddy's gambit.

"Does Tito know," I asked Olga, "that Stepan was Prince Paul's personal chef? Do you think Tito would like a quisling in his kitchen? What if he started cooking with arsenic?"

I kept the chef.

We'd hardly arrived in Valjevo when MacLean announced we'd have to get horses. I knew from the old days in Moscow how much Fitzroy liked to ride, but I wondered whether it was worth all the trouble and expense of fitting up a stable.

"Indeed it is," MacLean answered. "Horses are absolutely essential in case the Germans make another raid on us."

"But we've got jeeps now. Couldn't we escape in those?"

MacLean gave me a withering glance. "When the Germans are raiding," he explained condescendingly, "the Partisans invariably hide in the deepest forests where jeeps can't go. Besides, we don't have to *buy* horses. We simply requisition them. And anyway I need exercise if I'm going to keep fit. Come on, let's go see Arso's Supply Officer."

The Supply Officer soon produced a couple of diminutive animals that looked more like rabbits than horses, but by shortening his stirrups MacLean was able to keep his long legs off the ground.

That same day we had the horses saddled up for a "reconnoitre" in the hills. When the horses turned up they were accompanied by four 'teenage roughnecks also mounted and armed with tommy guns.

"What in God's name are those thugs for?" I asked.

"They aren't thugs, they're our bodyguards. Always have bodyguards when you leave camp, you know."

"What are we being protected from—wolves?"

"No, assassins," MacLean retorted.

We mounted up and trotted off into the wooded hills south of Valjevo. Behind us clanked the bodyguards, their tommy guns slung loosely across their chests. We came to a level sandy road leading through a forest of tall pines and prodded the horses into an uneasy gallop.

Suddenly a shot rang out behind me and I drew my head down between my shoulders as a bullet whined past my ears into the trees.

"Now what the hell?" I shouted and looked back at the bodyguards flopping precariously about in their saddles. One of them grinned gaily and pointed to his tommy gun.

"Trigger got caught on a button," he laughed.

From then on the bodyguards rode ahead of us. I was afraid assassins might try to ambush us, I told them.

Despite the fact that Supreme Headquarters had moved in, Valjevo stuck doggedly to its sleepy rural life. There was none of the bustle and noise of other big headquarters. Occasionally a column of Partisans marched through, their tommy guns slung over their shoulders, half-filled knapsacks hang-

ing on their backs. They knew they were headed for the
build-up for the Battle of Belgrade, but they were gay and
spirited as they swung through the tree-lined, dusty, cobble-
stoned streets, their heads thrown back singing old Serbian
army songs. Sometimes a mounted patrol would trot out from
the barracks to patrol the approaches to the town, for the
Germans were still in most of the big cities around us—some
only a few miles away. At any time they might sally out on
a quick raid and chase us off into the woods with their armored cars and tanks.

It was almost impossible to believe that all about us the
countryside was swarming with columns of troops—German,
Serbian, Russian and Cossack—headed toward Belgrade,
some to defend it, others to attack it, in a battle that was to
take the lives of thousands in only a few days time. Here in
Valjevo all was peace and calm. No staff cars, sirens blazing,
sped through the streets. No colonels with bulging briefcases
hurried from conference to conference. No motorcycle messengers broke the quiet with the unmuffled roar of their
engines. Here where the front was only a few miles away, in
any direction you chose, no one thought about "divisional
slices" and P.O.L. and PX's and Motor Pools. It was almost a
relief that a solid line of enemy troops along the Dalmatian
Coast and south across Macedonia separated us from the
Frankenstein armies of the West with their colossal staffs and
hordes of camp-following, overworked pay clerks and code
clerks and officious stenographers and M.P.'s. London seemed
another world—which I didn't want to see again until the
war was over and it had demobilized itself for good.

one

day MacLean and I had come in around noon from a long morning's ride to find our two missions in a high state of excitement. I asked Bill Callanan what was up. "Pokret," he said and darted back into the house.

"What the hell's 'Pokret?' " I asked MacLean. "The bubonic plague or an earthquake?"

"It's Serbian for 'Get going—the Germans are coming,' " Fitzroy explained. "Let's go and ask Arso what's up."

Arso and the Supreme Headquarters were living in a rattle-trap old wooden villa a couple of blocks away. As we hurried toward it a Partisan soldier riding a horse that looked like a hedge-hog galloped past us. "Pokret," he shouted as he threw us a polite salute.

We trotted into the courtyard of the villa to find a peasant cart in the process of being loaded. A soldier hurried out of the villa with a metal locker trunk on his shoulders. With a hunch of his back he heaved it over the side of the cart.

"Pokret," he shouted as he wiped the sweat from his forehead.

The trunk hit the floor of the cart. There was a cracking of planks as it plunged through the floor to the ground.

Arso's ADC dashed down the steps of the villa, a large typewriter in his arms.

Seeing us, he shouted "Pokret" and tossed the typewriter after the locker trunk. Plunging through the shattered wagon floor it hit the dust, manure, and cobblestones of the courtyard with a crash of metal and a jangle of bells. This was too much for the horses who leaped forward out the gate.

"Pokret," screamed the driver as he tugged at the reins. We never saw him again.

When we found Arso he explained he had decided to move headquarters to Arandjelovac, some forty kilometers nearer to Belgrade.

"The only trouble is we don't have any transport except horses," Arso told us. "Each of you British, Russians and Americans has a jeep, but we poor Partisans only have horses. If you start now you'll get there long before I do, which would be hardly proper seeing that I'm the Chief of Staff. Maybe you could lend us one of your jeeps. Otherwise I might have to ask you all to stay behind till we get there by horse."

We galloped over to the Russians with Colonel Huntington. None of us wanted to loan his jeep to any Partisan, particularly the Chief of Staff. Neither did we want to be left ignominiously behind. So we proposed a compromise: each of us would take one Partisan General in his jeep and one other Partisan on top of the baggage in his trailer. That satisfied Arso and we decided to move as soon as we finished lunch.

Stepan, our chef, had prepared an especially elaborate lunch that day and we were still in the middle of it when Arso and General Kisiliev of the Russian Mission drove up outside our billet and began blowing the horn of the Russians' jeep. We shouted out the window what was delaying us—a magnificent suckling pig. So Arso and Kisiliev came in and helped us finish it and eventually around three o'clock, well-fed and well-slivovitzed, Partisan Supreme Headquarters moved off. Stepan, by common consent, was strapped onto the last trailer. Quisling or no quisling, he cooked too well to be left behind. Later when I watched how an Allied Head-quarters moved from one town to the next with all its "staff-work" and reams of mimeographed instructions and time schedules, I recalled nostalgically with what simplicity, comfort and exhilarating confusion it used to be done in the Partisan Liberation Army.

The road to Arandjelovac, like all Yugoslav roads, was narrow, bumpy and very, very dusty. Since the Russian Mission Chief was a lieutenant general we couldn't dispute his right to go first. The British Chief, MacLean, had been breveted a brigadier. Colonel Huntington, though he had probably seen more professional service than either of the others and had battle stars for every battle we'd fought almost back to the French-Indian War, was, in pursuance of some sort of itchy inferiority complex that infects both War and State Departments, a mere colonel. So for forty kilometers we wallowed in the accumulated dust of Russia and the British Empire.

What with the dust, the bumps and the flat countryside, the Pokret was not particularly enticing. We were going east toward the Russian front, it is true, but the latest reports indicated we wouldn't make contact with the Red Army for some days. The gap between the Western Allied Command, of which we were a part, and the Russians, after three and a half years' fighting had narrowed to less than a hundred miles, but that hundred miles represented Germany's withdrawal route from the Balkans and the Mediterranean.

For several days, German divisions had been streaming through the gap from Macedonia and Bulgaria to take up positions in front of Belgrade. Partisan scouts reported that most of the towns to the south had been evacuated. The few Germans who remained were far too busy getting through the gap to waste time molesting a diminutive motor convoy of three jeeps. Nevertheless, we kept our revolvers handy and carried a couple of tommy-gunners on each of the the three trailers.

With each mile we travelled the gap seemed to grow smaller. Soon elements of the western command in Italy would be in physical contact with the Eastern Front. There was only one small fly in the ointment. Between us and AFHQ an army of Germans stood along the Dalmatian Coast. No matter how you looked at it, we were still an isolated command behind the other fellow's lines.

From time to time we met a few Partisan patrols plodding doggedly through the dust, bedraggled, dirty, obviously tired but alert and ready for a fight. Ten miles from Arandjelovac we met another mounted patrol going west. They, too, were dirty, tattered and weary. There were forty or fifty of them led by a single officer. At intervals in the column a rickety haycart filled with fodder and knapsacks creaked along. Just another Partisan patrol back from a reconnaissance, we thought. Most of them carried captured German camouflaged ponchos over their shoulders like any other Partisan.

Then I noticed something peculiar.

At first I couldn't identify it, but then I shouted to Huntington beside me, "Look, their caps are different. They've

Hammers-and-Sickles on them. Look at the medals all over
their chests. They're not Partisans, they're Russians!"

Up ahead General Kisiliev had already spotted his countrymen and brought his jeep to a stop. In a second, the
whole staff was out on the road shaking hands, embracing
and shouting at the poor bewildered patrol, thoroughly confusing even the Lieutenant in charge.

"But brothers," General Kisiliev shouted, "don't you recognize my uniform? I, too, am a Russian soldier."

They looked at his clean uniform and gold-braided epaulets and shook their heads skeptically. A Serb he might be,
but a Soviet general, no. All the generals were miles in the
rear, they murmured.

I, too, tried my hand and asked them where they were
from. "We've come from Stalingrad through Rumania and
Bulgaria," they answered. "But we're sorry we can't speak
Serbian."

"But I'm *not* talking Serbian. Can't you understand what
I'm saying in Russian?"

"No, sir, we can't. You see we don't speak Serbian at all."

"But you've understood what I asked you."

Gradually the dumb, uncomprehending faces began to relax. A young soldier back in the crowd shouted, "But sure,
comrades! That's Russian he's talking. He's an American—
our ally."

Their expressions gradually broadened into grins. They
swarmed forward all over us, fingering our uniforms and
equipment.

"Americans! We've joined up with the Americans!"

In another moment all hell broke loose. Bottles of slivovitz
appeared from the trailers. The Russians took liberal gulps
and grabbed the nearest "allies," kissed them on both cheeks,
and broke into wild dancing.

"*Amerikantzi! Anglichani! Partisani! Krasno Armeetsi*

(Red Army men)! We're all together. Hitler's licked and the war's all over!"

"Almost all over, Comrades," General Kisiliev warned. "There's still a bit of fighting to be done. We're together now and it won't be long before we're through. Now get on with your job. We've got a job to do, too."

The Lieutenant in command of the patrol took the hint, barked a few orders, and the Soviet soldiers fell into formation. We clambered back into our jeeps and slowly drove past the platoon, taking the Lieutenant's salute.

A half hour later we were in our new quarters in Arandjelovac. The Colonel told Sergeant Muselin to set up his transmitter at once and establish contact with base for an urgent message. There was a crash and a grunt outside the window of the room where Huntington, Callanan and myself were drafting and coding a flash to Washington that we'd linked up with Tolbukhin's Third Ukrainian Front. We looked out and saw Muselin lying on the front step where he had fallen from the roof in his hurry to rig up his aerial. But Muselin was a football player like Huntington and he knew how to fall. By the time we'd carried him to a cot beside his radio and had strung up the antenna for him he was ready to tap out our historic message.

When the excitement was all over and Bill Callanan and I had settled ourselves over a bottle of slivovitz, we began to wonder whether the day's dramatics were quite as world-shaking as we had thought. A half dozen stray Americans and British, hundreds of miles from base, with a sizable force of Germans between them and their lines, had run into a gypsy-like tribe of Russians from the Red Army. However, we came to the conclusion, as the level of the slivovitz dropped in the bottle, that one way or another October 18, 1944, was one of the historic dates of World War II. (On that same day Eisenhower and Montgomery were sitting in

Brussels planning for their winter offensive which was to have carried them to the Rhine. Between them and Zhukov's forces there were still more than five hundred miles of enemy territory. Then came the setback of the Battle of the Bulge. Not for more than six months were they to establish contact with the Russians at Torgau in the heart of Germany.)

Arandjelovac had been captured only two days before we arrived and there was plenty of evidence of street fighting: houses burnt out; walls blown in by artillery fire; most of the glass gone from the windows.

When we drove in, our convoy got a rather mixed reception. Crowds of townsmen and refugees from Belgrade lined the streets waving and shouting "Hurrah for the Russians" in what seemed a somewhat perfunctory manner. When the American and British jeeps were spotted, I thought I noticed a slightly more spontaneous enthusiasm. As soon as the convoy stopped in the main square, we were surrounded by curious crowds three and four deep. Questions were thrown at us in half a dozen different languages: Were we really Americans? Where did we come from? Were we going to stay a while? Could we take letters to uncles, aunts, sisters, brothers in Detroit, Pittsburgh, Chicago?

A young girl with a worried look pushed her way to the front of the crowd.

"Sir," she said to Colonel Huntington in fluent English, "can't you tell us what's going on? Since the war started we've been liberated by five different Yugoslav armies. Then the Germans, the Italians, the Russians and the Bulgarians. Now come the Americans and the British. Are you the last or must we expect still more armies to free us?"

Life was by no means unpleasant in Arandjelovac. We Americans shared a comfortable little villa on a hill behind the town. There wasn't too much work to do for the simple reason that Muselin couldn't handle much traffic on his small field radio. As there was no other way of getting reports out, it seemed rather senseless to write them.

Arso had told us Tito would be waiting for us in Arand-jelovac. But to our annoyance he wasn't there and never did come, so we confined our work chiefly to Order of Battle intelligence. Each morning we foregathered with our colleagues, the Russians, Partisans and British, and put together the information we had gotten from our field missions regarding this division or that battalion of enemy troops. Had the Prince Eugen Division pulled back from Nis? Had the 114th been moved from Croatia to the Venetian Front? Where was the 19th Panzer? How many Cossack divisions were the Germans equipping? Was a Green Triangle shoulder-patch a symbol of the First Mountain or the 117th or of some special formation? All the evidence we could fit together on these matters we radioed back to G-2 in Italy. After that, school was out for the day.

Colonel Huntington spent most of his spare time playing a sort of two-handed game of football with Muselin. Callanan joined me in endless arguments and discussions, from the Chetnik vs. Partisan debate to how many Trotskiist angels had sat on the point of a Stalinist pin. When the arguments got too bad, Bill would pull out his Shakespeare and I would take Serbian lessons from the landlady's children. (Today I've forgotten all my Serbian but Bill is writing plays for Broadway—which is as I should have expected it.)

But it didn't last long. At Supreme Headquarters (a slightly battered old villa occupied by Arso and his tiny staff) there was a growing atmosphere of expectancy. They talked of the "big push," the "final drive"; and the magic word "Belgrade" was whispered with increasing frequency.

Arso explained to us that four German divisions were stationed along the Danube east and southeast of Belgrade.

Parts of two other divisions were garrisoning Belgrade itself. Tolbukhin and his Third Ukrainian Front had crossed the Danube south of the Germans and four Russian mechanized divisions had pushed due west to the main international highway that runs directly south from Belgrade to Salonica. As soon as they reached the highway, they turned straight north to the city in an attempt to cut off the four German divisions stranded on the east of the road. The latter, Arso said, were very short of equipment with practically no ammunition for their heavy weapons, which they were abandoning, and hardly enough cartridges for their rifles.

However, he warned, Avala Mountain, which lies on the very edge of the international highway twenty miles south of Belgrade, was still in German hands. If they managed to hold it, they could keep open a gap in the north-south line through which the divisions in the east could retreat. In the advance north to Belgrade, Arso announced proudly, the Partisan First Corps would form Tolbukhin's left wing just west of the highway.

Having long since given up a strictly military career, I was looking forward to a few days relaxation in Arandjelovac until the generals had got done with their messy business. But Colonel Huntington, the old war-horse, thought otherwise. If there was going to be a battle, he was going to be there, and all the signs pointed to a very bloody battle indeed, the first really large scale, orthodox battle the Partisans were to get into. Unfortunately for Huntington, Arso would not hear of allowing any Allied Mission members anywhere near the battlefield. Huntington cajoled, pleaded, argued, threatened. But Arso was stubborn. MacLean threw in his weight, which was considerable in Partisan circles, but still Arso held fast.

As early as October 18, the Russians were well on their way north to Avala Mountain and Belgrade. On the nineteenth they by-passed Avala and had reached the outskirts of the capital. Two of the four German divisions on the Danube had struck north and west and had reached Belgrade where a single bridge across the Sava River offered an escape toward the northwest. But the other two, the Prince Eugen and the First Mountain, were caught in the trap. Four mechanized Russian divisions lay directly across their line of escape on the international highway. By this time the Germans' ammunition had run so short that they were being supplied by parachute drops, many of which were falling into Russian hands. There was nothing for it but to break through the Russian line behind them or surrender.

They chose the first course and during the night of October 19–20, armed only with hand weapons, the two German divisions stormed the highway where it skirted Avala Mountain. Along the highway, the Russians had lined up their field artillery, in some places hub-to-hub, charged with shrapnel and aimed at point-blank range. Behind them, in the forests west of the road, the Partisan First Corps lay hidden to pick up any Germans who might slip through the fine-meshed Russian net. The results were a foregone conclusion. By morning, the Partisans estimated that only a thousand of an original twenty thousand Germans had managed to run the gauntlet and cross the Sava. Nineteen thousand, they claimed, were killed or captured. The estimate was probably a bit high. But early the next morning, when we slipped from Arso's clutches and drove up the highway past Avala to Belgrade, we saw for ourselves what the slaughter had been.

All along the road as we approached Avala row after row of Russian field guns stood silently pointing eastward into fields speckled with German field grey. Beside the guns the exhausted Russian gunners lay sleeping after a busy night. The stench of gunpowder competed with the smell of new mown hay. It was strangely silent, calm—a ghastly pastoral.

Wherever you looked there were steaming, silent guns, sleeping Russians, dead Germans. From the woods west of us came the crackle of machinegun fire where the Partisans were cleaning up the remnants.

Guerrilla fighters can't always be expected to take prisoners because they have no means of caging them or feeding them as they move from one hideout to another. The Partisans had been bitterly criticized for shooting their prisoners. Each time they had answered their critics by promising that as soon as they fought on a stable front it would be different. Was it different now, we asked ourselves, as we heard those bursts of machinegun fire? In a field beside the road we passed a heap of German corpses. Perhaps two hundred of them lay sprawled in an area scarcely a hundred yards square. Had they been killed in battle or had they surrendered and been herded together before the machineguns were sprayed on them like garden hoses? Out of a small wood ahead of us a figure in field grey emerged, his hands high above his German helmet. As he limped down the slope toward the road, there was a brief burst of rifle fire and the German crumpled into the autumn clover. Around the next bend a soldier was standing with a smoking tommygun. He wore a Russian uniform.

The tattered Partisan soldiers were soon at work among the German corpses stripping them of their clothing and equipment, leaving them bloody, white, and naked under the glaring sun. As we drove along, the uniforms of the Partisan detachments changed from dirty rags to neat field grey. Baste sandles were replaced by heavy German army boots. Even the Germans' peaked field caps took the place of the ragged overseas caps of the Partisans—but not until the Red Star emblems had been torn from the discarded kepis and sewn to the caps.

A mile beyond Avala, Russian motor transport columns

blocked the road. Seeing that we were Americans, a young Soviet captain asked us to join him for a glass of milk in the farmhouse he'd taken over as a command post. With him were a couple of young lieutenants, one of them his unit's Politruk, or political advisor.

We asked how the Partisans had fought.

"Marvelously," said the Captain. "They're brave, shoot straight, know how to handle themselves and above all they never hesitate to put themselves under the command of any Russian who turns up, no matter what his rank. Of course," he added a little superciliously, "they're not as well trained professionally as our soldiers are, but they're damned good amateurs."

The discussion turned to the shooting of prisoners.

"Politically, of course, it is most unsound," the Politruk commented pompously, "but then you must consider the poor ignorant Serbian peasants who make up the Partisan army. They are uneducated, politically backward and utterly uncultured. They don't know about International Law the way we more civilized nations do." He graciously indicated that the British and Americans were included in this latter category. "Of course, it is wrong for them to shoot prisoners and now that they've joined up with us, we'll send them some political instructors to tell them how to behave."

This harangue failed to impress the Politruk's comrades. The Captain turned on him.

"Hey! Anton Antonovich, so only the Partisans shoot prisoners, eh? How many have you shot since Stalingrad? Or rather how many haven't you shot? Don't try to tell our American allies lies. When I found out that the Germans, when they came to our village, had hanged my father and raped and strangled my sister, I swore I'd never take one of those bastards prisoner again and I'm not ashamed to admit it. Have another glass of milk, Karl Georgevich," he said, turning to me. "It's fresh out of the cow. They must have been milking her while we were still shooting. Personally I'd prefer vodka. But you know the old proverb, 'When you don't have any fish, crayfish will do.' "

Eventually the traffic jam on the highway got untangled and, after hearty embraces and much backslapping, we climbed back into our jeeps. The Captain, who had come out to wave us on our way, pointed at Colonel Huntington's football which Sergeant Muselin was mothering in his arms.

"What the hell is that?"

"It's a football," I explained.

"A football? But it isn't round. What happened to it?"

I explained that there was a slight difference between American football and Russian soccer.

"That's one for the book!" the Captain laughed. "American soldiers take even their sports equipment to battle." He roared heartily and I think I detected a slight blush on Colonel Huntington's weatherbeaten face.

The next twenty miles to Belgrade were a seething snarl of Russian (made-in-U.S.A.) trucks, Partisan army wagons and peasant carts. But the drivers were good-natured and whenever they could they made way for us to weave past them. The road and the ditches continued to show horribly obvious evidence of last night's fighting.

Eventually we reached the outskirts of the capital and were told Partisan Headquarters had been set up in the fashionable suburb of Dedinje—a high ridge southwest of town overlooking the Sava River. The Partisans and Russians had been fighting a house-to-house battle with the German defenders, pushing them back until only a few strong points were left.

When we got to Dedinje the streets seemed strangely deserted. A sign pointed to First Corps Headquarters, but the building was deserted. A freshly made hole in the side of the house, obviously from an artillery shell, explained why. The whirr of another shell and the crash of its explosion a block away indicated that the Germans were taking a lively interest in the fancy villas of the stylish suburb. Discreetly, but without loss of time, our jeeps backtracked to the other side of town where we finally found Peko's Headquarters just as he and his staff were sitting down to lunch. They were in the highest spirits when we joined them. At long last *"Der Tag"* had come. Belgrade was in the process of being liberated and it had fallen to Peko's First Corps to do the job (with a certain amount of help from Tolbukhin's Army Group).

Again the conversation turned to prisoners and Peko, smiling charmingly, announced that First Corps had set up a prisoners' cage complete with barbed wire, guards, and all the fixings. While he didn't say so, it was obviously an innovation that the Partisans were really proud of. Now at long last they could behave like other armies. Not only had they practically liberated their capital, but they'd become respectable. (I wondered if they had noticed the example their big Russian brothers had set in the matter of shooting prisoners.)

In the middle of lunch a report came in that the Kalamegdan Fortress, the last German strong point in the city, was surrendering. Peko's Chief of Staff, a fellow called Penisich, jumped into one of our jeeps and we all dashed toward the Eighteenth Century fortress on the promontory where the Danube and Sava Rivers join.

The streets were a tangled mass of burned-out tanks, overturned trucks and trolley cars. Telephone and trolley lines formed weirs through which we had to weave our way. Not a building had escaped the house-to-house fighting of the past two days. Practically all the window glass was gone. Many houses were gutted. (Later we learned that much of the damage resulted from earlier American bomber attacks.) There'd been no time yet to hang up hammers and sickles and welcoming banners. The only slogan I saw read, "Capitalist

imperialism plus communism means death to small nations."
I wondered how long that relic of the German occupation
would survive.

The city was still under heavy shell fire from German batteries across the Sava and from time to time we came upon
a recent shell burst. Civilians, mostly old men and women, no
doubt relatives of the victims, stood about dazed and stunned
as soldiers carted away the mangled corpses. More shells
whined over the rooftops, but the populace was too be-
numbed by the events of the last forty-eight hours to pay
much attention. From behind the city a volley of Russian
Katusha rockets screamed across the Sava River, their glaring tails clearly visible even in the bright sunlight. Clouds of
black smoke and rubble marked the hits. Half a minute later,
the roar of the explosions carried back to us.

At the Kalamegdan Fortress the last German defenders
were being routed out, their hands above their heads. Except
for isolated individual soldiers hiding in cellars, German resistance had ended. Belgrade was "liberated."

Peko's Chief of Staff took us to the parapet of the fortress
overlooking the Sava River. A few hundred yards upstream,
the bridge to the west was badly hit but still standing.
Wagon trains and columns of foot soldiers were crawling
across it out of Belgrade. For a moment we thought they
must be the retreating Germans. Further up the river the big
railway trestle was a tangled wreckage in the stream. Just below it stood the stone pillars and approaches of the original
Alexander Bridge which the Yugoslavs themselves had blown
up during their gallant but futile resistance to Hitler's invasion in 1941. The steel bridge now teetering on its founda-
tions had been built by the Germans to replace it. Why they
had failed to blow it up when their last rear guards retreated
across a half hour before, no one could understand.

Later there were a dozen stories about it, each one more

exciting than the last: the demolition squad was made up of Austrians who refused to set off the charge and later surrendered to the Russians. A Partisan (Russian) soldier (civilian) had swum the river and cut the wires leading to the detonators. An old Partisan sniper had hidden in a hut near the bridge and, as the engineers were about to set off the charges, he had picked them off one by one with his rifle before he was surrounded and hanged by the German rear guard. (Having had a little experience in military affairs, I've always suspected that that famous military institution, the chain of command, had got clogged up just before the order to demolish the bridge came through.)

Whatever the real explanation, one thing was certain, the Germans hadn't left it standing on purpose. Hardly had the first Russian patrols reached the western bank when German batteries opened fire from behind the Zemun airfield. Most of the shots were wide of the mark, but a few missed the bridge only by inches. Meantime the Russian assault units were deploying in the sand dunes and marshes around the bridgehead. From our observation post on the parapet high above the river we watched the Russian advance units crawling from cover to cover dragging their light field guns behind them. A couple of hundred yards beyond them we could see the puffs of smoke from the guns of the German rear guard concealed behind a low embankment. Occasionally we could make out a German soldier crawling back from the embankment to the rear. Then a shell hit the bridge. It trembled, but remained standing. The advancing column stopped. Several horses, evidently hit by the shell, were shoved off the bridge into the stream together with the wreckage of their carts. Two human bodies followed them. Then the column crawled on.

I huddled with MacLean, behind a large stone lion on the parapet occasionally taking a peek over the lion's front paws.

MacLean was much braver and rested his field glasses on the lion's back to get a good look at what was going on. But the real lion was Colonel Huntington. For some reason, probably his haste to get going after lunch, he'd got his white-lined parka on inside-out, and could be spotted ten miles away.

I pointed this out to him, as respectfully as I could, but he said he had no time for changing. He intended to watch every move of the battle, plot it on his big white map, and even take pictures of it. He climbed on top of the parapet and held his map out in front of him. The Germans, see-ing the great white shape, must have thought he was in-viting a *pourparler,* and for some minutes they held fire.

Then the wind began to get the better of his map and he invited me to jump up beside him and help hold it. I climbed on the stone wall behind which I'd been so assidu-ously hiding. With the map under control, Huntington got his bearings and began to trace the movements of the troops below us. Meantime, just behind us a battery of Russian horse-artillery had unlimbered and were popping off noisily in the direction of the German positions. When Huntington had finished his map reading exercise, I excused myself as dis-creetly as possible and jumped back down behind the lion. Just about then, the Germans must have decided Huntington was not a truce flag after all. A couple of rifle shots spattered into the wall behind us. I began to get worried.

"Colonel, for God's sake come down from there. They're shooting at you."

I couldn't have said anything better designed to keep the Colonel on the wall.

"That's great! Haven't been under fire since 1918," he said in the same tone of voice he might have said, "Haven't had a better time since the Harvard game of '98."

The whirr of airplane engines rose above the shriek of the

Katushas and the banging of the Russian battery behind us. A formation of planes appeared above us.

One of the "orientation courses" I'd been assigned to, when I joined up in the OSS, was airplane identification. For several days I struggled with silhouettes without success. Then I explained to the instructor I was just a political soldier, and had no prospect or even intention of getting anywhere near the fighting front. These silhouettes were simply wasting my time. The instructor agreed readily enough and I went on to my next course. So I was always a little envious when my American and British colleagues would spot a speck in the sky and announce expertly:

"That's a B-26—converted for close camera work. You can tell from the way the left wing droops." Or:

"That's a Messerschmidt 298—latest model—see how the tail sticks out?" Or:

"That's a Yak-18—see how the propeller goes around the other way?"

All I know is an airplane when I see one, and since the flying saucer business began, I'm not even very sure of that.

So when my companions began to shout that the planes above us were Russian Yaks, I took their word for it. And when they cheered and said, "Now the damn Heinies are going to catch hell!" I cheered, too.

But when the planes began to peel off out of formation and dive straight at us I began to wonder. When the first load of bombs fell short of the bridge and landed at what seemed like my feet, I asked cautiously, "But if they're really Yaks, couldn't they be persuaded to go somewhere else?"

My companions frowned and looked embarrassed. The next load of bombs landed further away, straddling the bridge but not quite hitting it.

"You're sure, aren't you," I asked, "that they're really Yaks and not Messerschmidts?"

My companions snarled angrily: "Of course they're Messerschmidts. Couldn't see them properly before. Sun got in our eyes." By that time the planes had unloaded their bombs and disappeared over the horizon.

I was relishing my private triumph to the full when I heard Huntington's voice from the parapet above me.

"Got to take some pictures." He fumbled with his Leica. "I'm no good with cameras. They won't work for me. Confounded contraptions!"

A pause followed while he pushed and pulled at the various buttons and levers. Another couple of rifle bullets zinged past him into the wall behind.

"Charlie, you can work a camera. Saw you do it the other day. Come up here and take a couple of snaps. Get those Germans running over there." He pointed to a couple of microscopic running figures bent low behind the German embankment.

I chewed my lip and, feeling like William Tell's son, climbed cautiously onto the parapet beside the white-clad Colonel. I got the camera open and aimed it. A rifle bullet whined past. I swore it went between the good Colonel and myself, but he insisted it had missed us by three feet. "Still," he said graciously, "that's good shooting for five hundred yards."

The Russian Battery Commander came forward to where we were standing, saluted politely and addressed himself to Huntington:

"If you officers are acting as markers for the German artillery fire, you're doing an excellent job. May I suggest you take that God-damned white coat and get the hell out of here? Why don't you just hide some place till the snow comes? It won't be more than a month or two."

I translated only the substantive parts of the Captain's remarks, but it was enough for Huntington who looked as crushed as I'd ever seen him. Reluctantly he jumped down off the parapet just as another volley of rifle bullets kicked up a cloud of dust behind him.

Our tour of the city went on until evening. German shells from the Zemun batteries continued to explode sporadically but the Russians reported they'd soon have the Germans out of artillery range of the city.

Meantime column after column of Russian troops tramped down to the bridge. They had fought their way two thousand kilometers from Stalingrad and they knew the sound of battle when they heard it. They knew what the artillery and rifle fire ahead meant. There was no singing, no joking, as they plodded down the slopes to the river. When they got to the bridge, the target of a hundred German guns, they didn't pause but marched steadily up the shell-pocked approaches and along the swaying girder till they reached the opposite shore. There they unslung their rifles and unlimbered their cannon for action. It was obvious they'd done it a thousand times and could do it again in their sleep.

as darkness fell, the shelling of Belgrade subsided. Soon news came that the Germans were retiring from the Zemun suburb, and eventually the incessant bombardment ceased for good. Short of a successful counter-attack, the capital was safe.

We found billets on the edge of town and immediately put our radios into operation to transmit the big news to the west. While the operators were trying to establish contact, all hell suddenly broke loose east of town. Mortar shells, rockets, tracers, flares lit up the sky. Shrapnel tinkled on the streets and the roofs. Was this a counter-attack? Were we to be thrown out of Belgrade after all? We told the operators to stall on our messages but to keep contact with base. Putting on our tin helmets, MacLean and I went out to investigate. A piece of steel shrapnel hit the cobblestone street in front of me. I looked at MacLean.

"Do you think it is very safe being out in this hail storm?"

"Very safe, no," MacLean answered laconically. "Safe enough, yes."

We walked on. Fortunately, we hadn't gone far along the blacked-out street when we met a military patrol. They challenged us. We identified ourselves and asked where Corps Headquarters was located. They gave us a guide and in five minutes we were talking to Peko himself.

"What's going on, Peko?" MacLean asked. "Haven't heard such a row since the war began."

Peko looked a little embarrassed: "It's nothing serious I promise. It's just . . . well . . . you see the troops are . . . are just sort of celebrating."

"Celebrating! Good God! Using up all that ammo and supplies just to celebrate. It took us months to get that out here to you," MacLean protested.

"Well, we're doing our damnedest to stop it but the boys are in pretty high spirits. They know that now they're linked up with the Russians, they'll have all the supplies they need. It won't have to come from you any more."

The thrust went home and MacLean and I both winced. "We understand and will report what you've said to AFHQ. But just for your own sake you'd better make sure the Russians are in a position to supply you. We've been supplying Russia ourselves pretty substantially for the past few years. We hope they have enough to keep you going."

Having just participated in his first big operation side by side with the Glorious Red Army, Peko was a bit cocky. But he was a sensible fellow and saw the point quickly enough.

"I agree the troops are getting a bit wasteful and I'm doing my best to stop it."

We walked back to our quarters relieved at least that Belgrade was safe. But we didn't forget Peko's crack. It was no surprise and we both had warned our people that once Tito hooked up with the Red Army, things were going to be different. Just the same, the switch was a bit abrupt.

As the night wore on, the celebrations subsided. But within a few days they started up again in other forms: parades, speeches, banquets and exchanges of telegrams of congratulations.

On October 27 the Partisans put on a Victory Parade at the Belgrade stadium. The Russians, except for the Military Mission, remained aloof but all the Partisan bigwigs were there. Marshal Tito took the salute. On his right in descending order were the Chiefs of the three Allied Missions, Lieutenant General Korneev, Brigadier MacLean and myself. The Partisan First Corps with Peko in command had been transformed almost overnight. Instead of the ragged, tattered, dirty conglomeration of clothing they'd worn in the woods, they now appeared in snappy substantial uniforms. They sometimes didn't fit too well but they were all of the same pattern: the field grey of the German Army. Only the Swastikas were replaced by the Red Star. The former owners who lay out at Avala weren't going to miss them, but those Germans who filled the newly established prison cages probably found the gusty, cold October winds of Serbia a bit chilly. So the Partisans generously gave them their own discarded rags.

Marching past the reviewing stand, proudly saluting Tito, they seemed a little shaky on Parade Ground drill. But to those who'd watched them stumbling through the mountains single file in their early days, they must have offered a strange contrast in their new role as regular troops. At that moment I envied the men who had watched them develop over the years. But perhaps it was just as well I hadn't. Close association with them had produced in many that emotional attachment which sometimes leads to strange political judgments. In Yugoslavia especially, you needed all the detachment you could find.

So perhaps it was just as well to be a Johnny-come-lately. Besides, in these past few days I'd probably watched more fighting than many of my unfortunate colleagues who'd been incarcerated in the Pentagon since the beginning of the war. What's more, we'd been among the very few ever to have observed, freely, unhindered and unchaperoned, a Russian Army in battle.

As we stood in the reviewing stand watching the troops march past, those ubiquitous kibitzers, the photographers and movie camera operators, buzzed about. Even the rough and ready Partisan military police couldn't keep them under control. They made us pose in pairs, in groups, shaking hands, pointing grandly at the horizon.

"Photographers," Tito said turning to me, "are probably the worst dictators in the world." I took his word for it.

For reasons best known to itself, the Security Office of the O.S.S. insisted that our Mission to Yugoslavia was a secret, though it was mentioned daily in the press. No member, therefore, was allowed to tell his family where he was. Though it gave an added air of romance to the Mission, it didn't make much sense. But regulations are regulations and censors apply them. There was even a special officer in Italy assigned the task of writing each week to members of families of those stationed "in the woods," saying something like:

"You will be glad to know that———is well and happy though he is not in a position to write to you at the moment. He sends his regards."

Perhaps such letters gave comfort to the "folks at home." Personally, I'd have been scared out of my pants if I'd ever got one, and I made a point of telling the officer he could cross my family off his list of correspondents. They were used

to my going incommunicado from time to time. Somehow
or other I always surfaced in the end.

This time, however, despite the censors and security officers, I surfaced more quickly than usual. A couple of weeks
after the Belgrade Victory Parade, I got a letter from my
mother:

"I was delighted to see you looking so well in the newsreel
last night. Your Cousin Mamie visited there once before the
First War. She said it was lovely, but do be careful about eating uncooked fruits and vegetables."

After the parades came the banquets. The first one was
given on November 7, the Anniversary of the Russian Revolution, by Tito, thus putting the Soviet Military Mission's
nose slightly out of joint. "After all, it's our holiday. Why
can't we be hosts?" they said.

But Tito, wanting to be a little more revolutionary than
the revolutionists, insisted on giving the party and inviting
twenty or thirty of his close friends plus the three heads
of the Missions.

It was the first time I'd seen Tito except for our brief
meeting at the Victory Parade. He was wearing the elaborate new uniform he had brought back from Moscow: a wide-
lapelled, double-breasted grey jacket, sparkling with decorations. The heavy gold-braid oak leaf insignia of a Marshal
was embroidered on his sleeve. After four years of the toughest sort of campaigning he carried none of the extra weight
he later put on in the more sedentary life of a politician.
He was short, stocky and strong. As he moved about the big
reception room his step was as light and vigorous as an ath-
lete's. He greeted his guests with all the ease and simplicity
of an old world grandseigneur, his big deepset eyes sparkling, his tanned, round muscular face wrinkled in a gay
smile. In his hand he invariably carried a cigarette stuck

vertically in a small black, pipe-shaped holder. "Europe's handsomest dictator," an American girl journalist had called him, a description he only half disliked. Tonight he was at the top of his form, for there was nothing he enjoyed more than a good party.

We ran through the usual gamut of toasts and speeches. Some of the younger Partisan generals emphasized a little more than seemed necessary that the Soviet Army was the only one that mattered. But whenever MacLean or I looked too annoyed, Tito would smile amiably at us and shrug his shoulders, as if to say, "Boys will be boys!"

Among the guests at Tito's dinner was the Soviet soldier-poet Serge Simenov, the current rage in Communist literary circles. Simenov was a big, good-looking, sleek-haired smoothy whom I disliked from the start. His conceit, half pompous, half boorish, was evidently the result of the great popular success of his corn-filled verses. Latest reports from Moscow indicate, however, that he has not retained the earlier esteem the Kremlin's literary police-critics had for him. According to Moscow's *Literary Gazette* he has failed to portray the "new Soviet hero type." I don't know exactly what that means but I hope it will produce an improvement in Simenov's manners.

His most popular poem at the time was an appeal from a soldier at the front asking his wife to be faithful. "*Zhdi Menya*" it was called. "Wait for Me." It was not exactly original, but it was long and it pulled out all the emotional stops. As the evening wore on and the slivovitz began to flow freely, Simenov was prevailed upon without much arm-twisting to recite the poem. He was a good reciter and he gave it all he had. By the time he was through, the assembled company of warriors had their heads in their hands and tears were streaming down their cheeks. When he finished, there was a brief pause and you could hear sniffles from one end of the room to the other. Then from the head of the table, came a voice choked with sobs.

"Do it again, please, Comrade Simenov, do it again."

Simenov coughed, cleared his throat and was off once more: "*Zhdi Menya. . . .*"

The Slav soul flowed free that night.

The next night the Russians gave a belated November 7 celebration. Vodka, caviar, toasts and speeches followed the usual pattern. The atmosphere was a bit more restrained than during the evening before; you had the feeling that the Russians were giving their younger brothers an object lesson in table manners. A Russian playing the role of Emily Post is not very convincing and on the whole the party was a bit boring.

Then MacLean gave a party. It was a rip-roaring affair with hands across the sea and the caviar, and plenty of good cheer in the form of slivovitz, whiskey and a jazz band.

That left me with the ball. Thanksgiving was approaching and we decided it would make a good excuse. Since you can't have a banquet in Yugoslavia without a speech, I told my Serbian teacher that I'd have to know enough Serbian by Thanksgiving to give a dissertation on the Pilgrim Fathers. The Pilgrim Fathers weren't particularly relevant to the situation in Belgrade in 1944, but then neither was Thanksgiving for most of us. It was a rush order for the teacher but with a good deal of cramming, we managed to get something worked up. For anyone who knows Russian, the chief trouble with Serbian is that it's very largely Russian mispronounced. To learn to put the accent on the wrong syllable is easier said than done.

There were about a hundred guests at the banquet, Yugoslav generals, politicians, editors, foreign Mission chiefs, some foreign journalists and our own Mission. Tito begged off, but he designated Arso to represent him. (Arso, however, forgot to tell me he was representing the Marshal so I seated him fairly far down the table—as far down as I dared. After dinner he complained bitterly at the insult, but I explained I was no mind reader and, for a Chief of Staff, he had a damn good seat.)

Ivan Ribar, the President of the People's Republic, was guest of honor on my right. On my left was Lieutenant General Korneev, the head of the Soviet Mission, as the senior ranking foreigner. Korneev was one of the few Soviet generals who'd completed the Imperial Military Academy before the Revolution. He was an intelligent and cultivated officer with manners that he'd obviously learned before the current styles in Soviet drawing room behaviour had been set by Molotov and Vyshinski. But Korneev was old and unwell and I don't think he much enjoyed this assignment with his country cousins in Belgrade.

When at last the time came for speech making, I managed somehow to stumble through a long paean about the Mayflower and the Puritans and Indians and turkeys and corn. I even suggested a number of things we might possibly be thankful for. Then I read the President's (Roosevelt's last) Thanksgiving Day Proclamation in unintelligible dialects of the various languages represented and sat down in exhaustion.

Korneev, the Russian, turned to me:

"You know, young man, I've been here in Yugoslavia nearly a year and that's the first speech in Serbian I've understood."

Ivan Ribar, on my other side chuckled loudly. "Small wonder," he said. "He was speaking ninety percent Russian."

But there was worse to come. When Korneev's turn came, he asked me if I wouldn't translate his speech into English, as his interpreter's English wasn't good enough.

Thereupon the old General rose and delivered himself of a half hour summary of the works of Thomas Jefferson on the subject of revolution, quoting all the celebrated passages I should have learned. When it came time to translate, I managed to get the tree of liberty watered with the blood of fascists and then went on to render some of the strangest Jeffersonian prose ever heard. Fortunately only a few American journalists and my own staff realized the hash I was making, and they managed to keep civil tongues in their cheeks.

While all these festivities were taking place, the Military Missions were getting installed in the Balkan Hotel—before the war a near-first-class hotel. The Germans and the Russian "liberators" between them had rather messed it up but a few days work by labor units of collaborationists restored some kind of order. The British Mission took the second floor. We Americans took the third and the Russians the fourth. On the ground floor were the kitchens, restaurants, etc., which we shared. The Russian Mission itself had moved into the villa Tolbukhin had commandeered during his brief stay in Belgrade. So the Red Army used their floor of the Balkan as transient quarters for field officers on their way to and from the front.

I installed myself in a comfortable suite with bedroom, office and bath. The only trouble was that the hotel, like every other building in Belgrade, was unheated and the cold Balkan winter soon began to seep through the windows and under the doors. So we sent urgent cables for electric heaters and before long our base supply officer managed to find a few that worked on Belgrade's unpredictable current.

Another slight problem was our Russian neighbors.

Before the fourth floor was turned into quarters for field officers, it housed a small army of soldiers and non-coms who apparently had no other mission than the agreeable one of having a very fine time, Russian Army fashion. This consisted chiefly of drinking all the alcohol they could find and then casting off all inhibitions. One of their earlier pranks was to steal into my room in the middle of the night while I was writing a report and let fly with a burst of automatic rifle fire at my precious electric heater. When I had recovered my nerves and started to remonstrate, they explained good naturedly that they didn't like things that glowed red in the dark. It was apparently an old Red Army phobia. They apologized, however, for having startled me. They hadn't known that American soldiers jump so when you fired off a machine-gun behind their ear. They promised they wouldn't do it again and offered to fix the heater. But they were obviously a forgetful lot for two nights later they did do it again, destroying the second of our two heaters.

So I went to my friend General Kisiliev, General Korneev's successor as head of the Russian Mission. It was a fine thing, I said, to have friendly relations but friendliness demonstrated by keeping you awake all night and shooting out your heater was overdoing it. Kisiliev agreed. I said I'd thought of putting an armed American guard on the door of my office but I was very much afraid it might lead to killing and that only caused trouble. So Kisiliev said he'd get the playboys moved from the hotel and in the meantime station a Soviet guard in my corridor to protect me from his roving drunks.

Ten years before, in Moscow, I had gone to every length I knew simply for a chance to talk with Russians. Now after two weeks of complete freedom to talk to them, I had to ask for armed guards to shoo them away.

Within a few days the playboys moved out and the officers moved in. The guard was also withdrawn. The officers didn't get quite as drunk as the soldiers and they didn't shoot as much, but they made up for both by talking. They soon learned there was a Russian-speaking American around and they lost no time in looking me up and then pouring out their pent-up souls.

An elderly major was one of my first callers. Thin, dark, nervous and ill-at-ease in his tightly buttoned uniform, he introduced himself as a scientific worker from Kharkhov. Then he began to talk in a strained, low tone.   .

"You'll excuse me for butting in like this," he started, "but I heard you spoke Russian and for two days I've been trying to screw up enough courage to talk to you. In fact I finally had to take a few little vodkas before I was brave enough to knock at your door."

He smiled apologetically as I showed him a chair and offered him a cigarette.

"What can I do for you?"

"Oh nothing, really. That's the hell of it. You Americans can't really do anything for us." He raised his hands in a gesture of helplessness. "But if you will just listen for a minute or two it would help. We Russians are really in a tragic mess. We have to let off steam and yet there is no one to talk to. You know how it is in Russia. If you hear something unpleasant you have to tell the police, just in case it was a police agent who told you. You can't blame anyone for informing. You have to inform to survive."

The Major dragged at the cigarette in short strong puffs, his eyes on the glowing ash. I waited for him to go on. Finally he pulled himself together and started with a rush.

"First, then, you must understand that, though I'm a Jew, I'm first of all a patriotic Russian. I love my countrymen no matter what their nationality. For them I will fight gladly and I'll even die gladly if I have to. You must understand that. I'm not a traitor."

His voice rose insistently as though he were trying to convince himself that in talking to me he was not committing treason.

"But it's the unnecessary killing and dying that I can't get used to. Soldiers have to die, I suppose. But old men, women, children, they don't have to be shot or starved to death, or worked to death, or simply harried to death. You know people can die inside and go right on breathing and slaving. That too is happening every day at home. Sometimes, in fact mostly, they don't even know they're dead themselves."

"Are you sure they're dead?" I interrupted. "Perhaps only a part of them dies, a useless part. Perhaps the part that stays alive is the important part. Think of all the people in Russia who really seem happy. Think of the May Day parades when the young people dance and sing and laugh as they parade past Lenin's Tomb in Moscow. Perhaps they are happy and perhaps that's the most important thing." (It was a phoney argument I'd heard used by fellow travellers and I wanted to know his answer to it.)

"No, no," the Major protested. "That isn't the important thing—that's just like drunkenness. It's hypocritical, like everything else Stalin starts." He paused as though shocked by his own blasphemy.

"Take just one example," he went on, "just one small part of his attitude—the way he treats my people and the other minorities. You know what I mean—his so-called nationalities policy."

I had once written a long report to the State Department on Stalin's nationalities policy. Stalin became an expert on minorities when Lenin, way back before World War I, had told him to write a paper on how the Communists would treat minorities when they came to power. The result was a singularly dull, uninspired essay but, probably because it was good politics to have a member of the Georgian minority

like Stalin sponsor the program, Lenin had published the
essay and added it to the dogma of Communist faith. When
eventually Stalin came to power he was faced with the problem of carrying it out. The result had not been a consistent
success—at least from the viewpoint of the national minorities themselves.

"What happened to us?" the Major continued. "They said
we could have our folk dances, and folklore and songs and
our costumes—if we could get the materials to make them.
They said we were autonomous and could even secede from
the Soviet Union if we wanted. A few central Asians took
that literally—and got shot for the mistake. The rest of us
played it more cautiously. After all, he had a couple of Jews
in his cabinet. He even married the daughter of one."

The Major paused and lit another cigarette. "This is
nothing new to you perhaps but I've got to tell someone—to
get it off my chest." He got up and started pacing around the
room.

"Autonomy meant one thing: We could sing, dance, write
poetry and talk in our native languages as long as the singing and poetry and talking didn't cross the Party Line. But
you know as well as I that the Party Line prescribes everything—how to work, how to play, how to love and hate, how
to marry and divorce, how to have children—and yes by God!
how *not* to have children. Which leaves us what? Not very
much."

The Major sat down, pulled a handkerchief from his
breeches pocket and wiped the saliva from the corners of his
mouth. Then he went on in a calmer tone.

"For a time we Jews had good luck. We've got more brains
than most. We could add and subtract and keep accounts.
Many of us went into the Army where for a while there
was no difference between Jews and Christians. But then
something happened, about the time Stalin fired Litvinov,

his Jewish Foreign Commissar. Perhaps Stalin was just appeasing Hitler, but from then on we Jews began being skipped over for promotions. Officers who snubbed us in the mess weren't punished any more. We were gradually shifted from combat branches to administrative jobs. I'm an expert artilleryman but today I'm a regimental supply officer.

"Can I get back into combat service? No! Can I practice my profession as an artillery officer? No! Can I get a promotion? No! And why? I'll tell you why: because Stalin's afraid. First he sacrificed us because he was afraid of Hitler. Now he's afraid we know it. And the fact is we do know it!"

The Major stopped and stared at me waiting for a reaction. But there was nothing for me to say.

"I'm sorry to bother you with all this," he said apologetically, "but you're an American. There are lots of Jews in America and they ought to know that all this business about Jewish equality in Russia is nonsense. Tell them that the only difference between Stalin's anti-semitism and Hitler's is that Stalin is smarter. You know the old saying 'Two Jews Equal One Armenian; Two Armenians, One Georgian'—and Stalin is a Georgian. Tell your Jewish friends that. And now I must go."

The old Major rose abruptly from his chair, shook my hand, bowed stiffly and walked out before I could stop him. He never called again.

Sometimes the nocturnal conversations with the men on the fourth floor went the other way. In those cases my visitors were generally younger men who had never known any other government but the Soviet. Their motive in talking to me was usually curiosity.

Since the war had started, they'd come into contact with American planes and trucks and particularly jeeps and canned food. Any country that could produce a jeep and such magni-

ficent canned stew was worth learning about. Couldn't I tell
them more? Obviously Americans must be wonderful people
or else they'd never have helped Russia so generously. American democracy was probably a little different from Soviet democracy but it was democracy of a kind. Could I explain a
little about it? They'd heard, for instance, that most American families had cars. But America was a capitalist country
and that means a certain, er . . . "exploitation if-you'll-
excuse-the-expression" of the workers. How could it be,
then, that workers had cars? But it always came back to the
jeep. Who invented it? Did he get a medal or a premium for
it? Or did he just make a lot of money?

I'm inclined to think that the genuine admiration for
America entertained by almost all Soviet soldiers I met was
inspired more by the mud-penetrating qualities of the jeep
than by anything else. The Kremlin's propagandists have
tried to counteract this by claiming the jeep was a Russian
invention. During the war, I can't recall a single Soviet soldier who fell for that line. To them the jeep was American.
In fact, it *was* America.

Among my callers was a Russian colonel from Leningrad.
He came into my office one evening after he'd had a snort or
two and sat for three hours recounting his troubles. He'd
been a lieutenant on the new German-Russian border when
the war broke out. For weeks Russian agents had been bringing reports of the build-up on the other side of the frontier.
With his own field glasses he could see the German tanks,
the motorized artillery, the observation planes, maneuvering
a few hundred yards from the Russian positions. Before the
Stalin-Ribbentrop Pact, troops on frontier duty always had
three weeks' supply of ammunition, gasoline, and food in
their dumps and were always on the alert.

But after the Pact, he said, Stalin had apparently been hyp-
notized by Hitler. First, the border troops were taken off the

alert and put on normal status. Then their ammunition supplies were reduced to a week's, then to three days' supply. Then orders were received to pull all mechanized units back ten kilometers from the frontier. Along the border itself, only patrols with light arms were allowed to operate. Soviet anti-aircraft guns were forbidden to fire at any strange aircraft lest it cause trouble with Hitler. And Soviet aircraft had been forbidden to fly within twenty kilometers of the frontier lest they, too, provoke the Germans. So for weeks they sat there watching the Germans putting more and more units on the front line ready to go.

As he described the situation the Colonel became more and more agitated. I offered him a cigarette to calm him.

"How could anyone but a fool or a traitor trust Hilter like that? And yet Stalin did. As a result, his whole first line of troops were sacrificed."

I remembered sitting in Moscow just before those days in June 1941. From our reports we knew Hitler was building up his strength in Poland for a massive attack. But when the fatal day came a good percentage of Russian officers were on vacation in the Crimea, and, as the Colonel said, their defenses had been whittled away to nothing.

The attack came early Sunday morning June 22, 1941. The Colonel went on: "The Germans had spotted our supply depots long before, by observation planes which had been allowed to fly over Soviet territory to their hearts' content."

The first German air attacks completely knocked out the supply system. Then within a matter of hours, the Russian artillery had shot up all their reserves of ammunition. There was nothing for it but to withdraw, leaving masses of Soviet infantry to hold up the Germans with nothing but hand grenades and tommyguns. But they were soon killed or captured and the armored units had been overtaken.

"The withdrawal," the Colonel said, "was a rout. In fact,

it didn't really stop until fresh units, newly equipped and supplied, had been formed up in front of Moscow.

"If only Stalin had given us a chance from the beginning we might at least have retreated in some sort of order. As it was, Stalin had his best-trained troops destroyed because he thought he could appease Hitler. It was worse than Munich. In three short months after June '41 we lost nearly four million in dead and prisoners, including some of our finest soldiers!"

At last the Colonel got up to go and apologized for taking so much of my time. It was already three in the morning and he had to start back to the front at five. He'd take the liberty of calling on me again when he got his next leave in four weeks' time, provided the Germans didn't get him. But he had a feeling that his time was up. It didn't really matter. In fact, it would probably be better that way. He had to fight for his country, but he had no great desire to go back there after it was over and live under the Politburo.

Two hours later I woke to find the Colonel sitting on the edge of my bed. He was now in battle dress. His kit bag was slung over his shoulder.

"Excuse me," he apologized, "for disturbing you again like this. But it occurred to me you didn't know who I was and you might have thought I was just a drunken officer who talked too much. You see, I'm completely sober now, and everything I said last night is true, terribly true. You must believe it and your people must believe it. Someone must know the truth about that great military genius, Stalin." His voice rasped with sarcasm. "I couldn't go back to the front suspecting that you would just dismiss last night's conversation as a drunkard's prattle."

With that he kissed me on both cheeks in good Russian style, got up, saluted and went out. I never saw him again either.

the

first few days of "liberation" were exciting ones for the Belgraders, but not always pleasant. The Red Army front had moved north out of earshot but not out of mind. Soviet supply trains and reenforcements continued to move through the city all day long and at night trigger-happy Soviet patrols toured the town shooting at anything that moved.

A day or two after we'd got installed in our quarters, a couple of our officers went out to see the night life. When they hadn't returned by one in the morning we were a little worried but both had had long experience "in the woods" and we figured they knew how to take care of themselves in the big city. They eventually showed up the next morning looking a bit bleary-eyed and sleepy.

"Where did you spend the night?" we asked.

They looked rather sheepish.

"In a gutter about five hundred yards from here."

"What happened?"

"Well, we just went out for a little stroll after dinner and started up the street toward the Parliament Building when a Soviet sentry hollered 'Stoi.' We answered with the usual 'friend' in Serbian but I guess those Russians don't understand Serbian very well. When we started forward again a burst from the sentry's tommygun hit the cobblestones beside us. Thank God, it was dark and he couldn't see what he was shooting at. He must have aimed at the sound of our voices. I wish I'd been brought up as a ventriloquist. We flopped into the gutter and lay there for a while."

"And then?"

"Well, after a few minutes, we called to him and explained we were 'soyuzniki.' That's the Russian word for 'allies,' isn't it? But he didn't take to that either because he just let go with his tommygun again, over our heads this time.

"After another half-hour or so we tried to crawl back away from our murder-loving friend but by this time he'd strolled quite close to us and he heard us wriggling and hollered 'Stoi' again. So we figured we'd better just lie still and like it. It wasn't too uncomfortable. After a while we must have fallen asleep. When we woke up, it was getting light and we could see the sentry just about fifteen yards away asleep on a doorstep. So we got up and gently walked away."

After that we made it a rule not to go out on foot after dark until the Red Army had moved on and the job of patrolling was turned over to the Partisans who were a bit more reasonable.

From the first day of "Liberation," Partisans had started taking over guard duty in public buildings. One of the first buildings I visited in Belgrade was our old Embassy office, to

see how it had survived the last three years. The offices were
in a five story building on the main street. Looking up at the
windows from the sidewalk, I noticed a broad red stain on
the wall that reached from a fourth floor window almost to
the street. I went inside and found a Partisan guard stationed
at the entrance. After I'd told him who I was he let me in,
explaining that I'd find everything in good order as the old
caretaker of the premises had remained on duty until the
very end of the fighting.

". . . Or almost till the end. He seems to have got a bit
too curious though and stuck his head out a window up on
the fourth floor just as the Germans were pulling back. I
guess someone—a German or a Russian—took him for a
sniper and pinged him through the head. His body was still
hanging over the window sill next day when I was sent here.
Perhaps you saw the blood down the front of the building."

The bloodstain remained as long as I was in Belgrade. But
on my last trip back, I was glad to see they'd managed to
scrape it off or paint it over.

The Partisan guard explained that he'd been posted in the
building just as soon as the fighting had passed beyond it.
"So no one has had much of a chance to steal anything," he
said reassuringly. "The only people I let in were from a Russian clean-up squad. They searched it just yesterday pretty
thoroughly so I don't think you'll find any Germans in it
any more."

In the first onslaught of Russian troops into the city, the
fighting had been so bitter, the resistance so stubborn, and the
advance of the Russians so fast, that not a few German soldiers fighting from house to house and room to room found
themselves trapped in buildings behind the Russian advance.
Obeying the Fuehrer's orders not to give ground, they had
allowed themselves to be by-passed in attics and cellars and
eventually surrounded by Red Army troops. Knowing the

Russians' aversion to taking prisoners alive, they sneaked down into the deep basements of Belgrade's old houses and there they hid in coal bins and root cellars and sewers and wells, while the Russian clean-up squads searched the houses. After a day or two, hoping that the Russians' vigilance had relaxed, or unable to withstand the thirst and hunger and cold of their dark hiding places, they would slip out from the cellars and try to find some unguarded alley through which they could sneak out of the city into the woods and from there, if they had any luck, across the Sava back to their own lines.

The Germans knew what kind of fighters the Russians and Partisans were, and they must also have known how slim were their chances of escape. Yet they knew, too, that the weaker they grew from lack of food and water, the slimmer those chances became. On those first nights we often woke to the rattling of machine-gun fire and the short quick cracks of German Mausers answering back, fighting like rats in a corner. How many Germans ever made it is hard to say. I never heard of a single one.

While I was inspecting the Embassy offices, a commotion arose in an old building across the main street. According to the signs over the first floor shop windows, it had once been a shoe store. But the shoes had long since disappeared from behind the shattered show-windows. Crowds were milling about the house. In the upstairs windows terrified apartment dwellers shouted half hysterically down to a platoon of Russian soldiers covering the two street entrances. Peering from our windows directly across from them, our Partisan guard explained to us that someone had seen two German soldiers hiding in the cellar of the house opposite. The Russian patrol had come to flush them out. Six days had already passed since the Russians had overrun the city—six days without food or water in a dark, cold, damp cellar. In front of each

entrance were a dozen tommyguns at the ready, a dozen itch-
ing fingers on a dozen hair-triggers.

Someone shouted in broken German to come out.

*"Kommen Sie 'raus. Kommen Sie 'raus. Wir schiessen
nicht!"* (We won't shoot.) Judging from the look of those
crouching tommy-gunners, I wouldn't have put much money
on that promise.

Nothing happened. A soldier ripped the sidewalk grating
from a basement window.

"Kommen Sie raus order wir werfen ein Granat."

Silence. The platoon leader unbuckled a hand grenade
from his belt, pulled the pin and tossed it through the basement window.

There was a loud explosion in the cellar, followed by a
muffled shriek. A cloud of dust and smoke billowed out the
window and the two doors.

The crowd stirred. "They're in there all right. I heard one
scream," a woman's voice shouted. An uneasy murmur ran
through the crowd. The tommy-gunners squatted lower, their
guns aimed at the cellar window. The onlookers pulled back
across the street out of the way.

Then from one of the doors tottered two bedraggled, half
naked figures. Their field grey breeches left no doubt they
were Germans. Blood streamed from their faces and their
naked torsos. One held both his hands high as he stumbled
forward blinded by the sunlight. The second man tried to
hold one arm up; the other hung helpless from a mangled
shoulder. The grenade had obviously done its stuff. As they
swayed out onto the sidewalk, the twelve tommy-gunners
squeezed their fingers. For a split second the guns crackled.
The two half-naked figures doubled up and sprawled on the
sidewalk. A gasp came from the crowd, followed by complete
silence.

The platoon commander barked an order. The Red soldiers fell into formation. Another order, and they marched off down the street leaving the two bodies where they'd fallen. A few moments later two Partisans appeared pushing a handcart. They lifted the bodies gently into the cart and trundled away after the Russians. Silently the crowd broke up. Before long there was nothing left but a puddle of dark red blood on the sidewalk.

Though they had good reason to be trigger-happy, by and large the Russian troops were correct with the Allied Missions, provided they knew who we were. If we persisted in going out after dark or didn't make ourselves known, there might be trouble. I always felt that there was an ill-disguised feeling of contempt in their attitude toward the clean, neat, well-equipped, well-turned-out Anglo-Saxons. There may have been a touch of envy too. There was never much old world courtesy about them. The Partisan soldiers, in the early days before they met their big Russian brothers, were very careful about saluting Allied officers. But I have yet to be saluted by a Russian soldier except at some formal ceremony. It was always a bit awkward when you met junior Soviet officers or soldiers on the street. You couldn't exactly salute them until they'd saluted you, but to stare at them and do nothing while you waited for the salute that never came, made you feel that you were as oafish as they were. So MacLean and I generally nodded amiably whenever our paths crossed, as they did frequently in our tramps around the city.

MacLean was a fiend for exercise and every day after lunch he'd take off on a two-hour walk through town or a horseback ride in the country around Belgrade. Personally I've always believed in siestas, but MacLean said it wasn't military to sleep after lunch. One afternoon we'd been exploring one of the older sections of Belgrade, twisting in and out of the narrow streets that separate the dilapidated old houses. We turned up one little street just as a Soviet major was coming down the other side followed by the ubiquitous orderly carrying a suitcase. We glanced at the major and nodded. The Major stopped and called out to us, "Gentlemen, in your Army don't you generally salute a superior officer?"

We stopped and crossed over to where he was standing.

"Why yes, always," MacLean replied politely.

"Then why, might I ask, did neither of you render me the courtesy of a salute?"

"Well, you see, Major," MacLean explained with exaggerated simplicity. "It just so happens that I'm a general, my companion is a lieutenant colonel and you're only a major."

The Major looked at our rank insignia, which he obviously didn't understand, and hesitated a brief second.

Then, with a grin from ear to ear, he snapped to attention, turned out a parade ground salute and put out his big paw in apology. Behind him the little orderly dropped the heavy suitcase with a thud, gave a stiff salute and held it till we had gone on our way.

But what bothered us most about the Russians was their attitude toward our jeeps. The trouble with a jeep in wartime is that there isn't a soldier or officer who doesn't want one. Besides, there is absolutely no effective way of locking it, or "immobilizing" it, as the dreadful official expression goes, so that some ingenious soldier can't un-immobilize it at his pleasure. You can take parts out of the engine, you can chain the steering wheel and the brake and the gear-shift with a dozen half-nelsons but still, if you turn your back for a couple of minutes, it'll be gone. In the early days when the Russians were on the loose in Belgrade, you couldn't even leave your jeep with a Partisan armed guard, of whom we had a dozen or so attached to each Mission. The Partisans had been so well schooled to believe their big Russian brothers were perfect, that if a Russian soldier came along and said he needed our jeep for urgent business, the guard would usually help him take it away. When we complained, the guard would say in all innocence, "But a Russian soldier said he needed it."

Once or twice we managed to find our jeeps by scouring the town looking for the various numbers and identifications that distinguished one jeep from another. But the Russians must have soon set up a special converting shop where they could paint out the old numbers, paint in their own and drive off, to all appearances the proud new owners of the jeep.

We hadn't been in Belgrade more than a week when I had to radio that our jeep convoy of three had been reduced to one. I got back a stern message quoting regulations about what happened to people who left jeeps "un-immobilized" in the Mediterranean Theater, of which we were a side-show. What the regulations did not say, however, was how to immobilize a jeep short of tossing a hand grenade into the engine. People who write regulations about jeeps obviously ride in staff cars.

MacLean had been having trouble with his jeeps too, so we decided strong measures were necessary. We requisitioned a small underground garage right across the street from our quarters and asked Partisan Headquarters to provide us with a guard properly indoctrinated about the rights and privileges of Allies to keep their jeeps, even if the Russians did want them.

For a day or so this worked very well and we congratulated ourselves on having outwitted the Red Army Jeep-Stealing Brigade. But the Brigade had not given up and soon discovered our hiding place.

One morning as I was dressing I looked out the window and saw the hunched-up body of a Russian soldier lying at the entrance of our garage. Later our Partisan garage guard, a tough, bearded, old peasant, told us that during the night a couple of Russians had demanded to be let into the garage. When he refused, they started to unsling their tommy-guns. So he shot one and the other ran off. We congratulated the guard, gave him some cigarettes and reported the matter both to Partisan Headquarters and the Russian Mission Chief, General Kisiliev. The latter didn't seem much concerned about his dead soldier, but apologized profusely for any slight inconvenience the incident might have caused us, and invited us both to dinner that very night as a gesture of contrition.

The dinner was the genuine Russian type, for Kisiliev, besides being very friendly, was very Russian, too, and because of ulcers he had been spared much of the front-line service that had roughed up the edges of so many of his fellow officers. His ulcers, however, didn't prevent him from drinking when the occasion demanded. That night the occasion apparently did demand. So we all poured the good Moscow vodka freely and gorged ourselves on iced caviar fresh from Rumania, vowed eternal friendship, and denounced Jeep Stealing as Trotskyist deviationism.

It was after midnight when the two of us returned to our quarters. As we turned into the garage we were surprised to find the doors standing open. Driving down the ramp, the lights of our jeep lit up the body of our Partisan guard lying in a pool of blood in the middle of the floor. We lifted the old fellow onto a bench and felt for his pulse, but it was obvious he'd been dead for some time. Two jeeps were missing.

Trembling with rage, we raced straight back to the Russian Mission. Kisiliev was already in bed, but we got him up and told him what had happened. He looked chagrined, and promised he'd replace the two jeeps in the morning.

We explained that the jeeps didn't concern us nearly as much as the shooting of the old Partisan guard. Kisiliev might take the killing of his soldier as lightly as he wanted, but this guard had worked for us. He'd been loyal and had done his duty, even to the extent of getting shot for it. Jeep stealing, we pointed out, was a damn nuisance but murdering people in the process was a hell of a lot worse, and until the Russians got a bit more control over their troops, they'd better keep them in barracks or out of Belgrade.

Kisiliev got the point, but explained that he personally had no operational command over any Soviet troops other than his immediate Mission. Nevertheless, he promised to call the attention of Tolbukhin to the behavior of his troops and see if something couldn't be done about it.

We imagined we saw a little improvement in Red Army manners after that, but it was probably the natural result of the front's gradually moving away and Tolbukhin's line of communication to Russia shifting northward through Rumania, by-passing Belgrade.

Jeep stealing was not the only extra-curricular activity of the Red Army. There was looting, robbery and rape, and rumors of looting, robbery and rape. How much there actually was, is hard to say, though the local population worked itself up to a high pitch with the horror stories it told itself. The Red Army political officers had been very active in trying to explain to the man in the ranks that Yugoslavia was a liberated, friendly country and that the Yugoslav's were their little brothers—albeit rather naïve, uncultured little brothers. Some of this must have made some impression on the troops and I'm inclined to think that the looting and rape were less in Yugoslavia among the Russians in Tolbukhin's command than they had been in the conquered countries. But Tolbukhin had a large proportion of Central Asian troops, too, Mongols, Kazakhs, and Turki. What they did on their nights off was nobody's business.

The similarity of languages too made a difference. There

is nothing that quite so infuriates a drunken Russian soldier as not being understood. Though the Yugoslavs could hardly carry on a conversation in Russian about dialectic materialism, they could generally get the drift of what a Russian soldier wanted—wine, watches, women. If they were shrewd, they could often satisfy them without getting shot in the process—or worse.

The Russians' behavior offered a strange contrast to that of their "uncultured," "ignorant" country cousins. According to people who'd been with them from the start, the Partisans had lived the most puritanical existence since the very first days of the resistance. Occasionally they went in for some collective folk dancing, when they linked arms around a bonfire and danced to the tune of an accordion or fiddle. They were even allowed to have a drink or two, especially when invited by the foreign Military Missions. But sex and drunkenness were rigidly tabooed and they lived up to their high standards with amazing discipline. In fact, some of our allied staffs found the Partisans' standards just a bit too high for their own tastes and fretted considerably at the strait-laced lives they were forced by Partisan example to follow in the woods. The romantic atmosphere of the forest, they felt, should not have gone completely unexploited.

Once we reached Belgrade a gradual relaxation was permitted in such fleshpots as the capital provided. Even then Partisan behavior was a good deal better than that of most armies.

But the tavern keepers of Belgrade were not yet aware of the peculiarly puritanical behavior of Tito's troops. Accustomed to frequent changes in the nationality of the occupying troops, they merely hid their bottles when they saw the storm brewing and waited for the changeover from Germans to Partisans to be completed. When quiet settled down again, they pulled out their bottles, hung out their shingles and waited for the Partisans to come in and make merry.

At that point Tito and his staff were too busy trying to organize a national government to worry about a few odd night clubs, so for a day or two Belgrade was wide open. We'd hardly been in the city two days when we heard that the famous pre-war café, the Russian Tsar, was doing business again. That afternoon MacLean and I went over to investigate. We found our way through a maze of passages, steep stone staircases and thickly curtained doorways to a large underground restaurant crowded with guests, a band blaring and the dance floor packed with well-dressed young men and women. From the moment we appeared in our unfamiliar allied uniforms, it was obvious we were not wanted. The headwaiter officiously told us that unfortunately all the tables were taken. We pointed to a table in a corner where a crowd of sleek, well-dressed 'teenagers were making merry. Here was Belgrade's "neutral" society having its last fun before hell broke loose for it.

When Hitler invaded the Balkans in 1940, there developed, in addition to the Chetniks and Partisans, a third camp of Yugoslavs, the Quislings, collaborationists and the "neutrals." Many of the last group never actually worked with the Germans. They simply stayed home and minded their business. For the most part they were the sons and daughters of the richer tradesmen, bankers, and professionals, who considered Tito anathema and Mikhailovitch a do-nothing Quixote. They elected to stay on in Belgrade and wait to see who won. When Tito won, they realized soon enough that their goose was cooked. But it was too late then to do much about it. So they put on their best suits and party dresses and set out to have a good time until Marko Rankovitch's police called to invite them to a labor camp or jail. Though they had committed no crimes, still they didn't inspire much respect or affection among us and we weren't going to let them keep us standing about for long.

"You'll clear that table for us at once," we told the waiter sternly. The waiter caught the hint, and in a few minutes we were comfortably seated over a glass of beer. The band went on playing, the golden youth continued to dance but there was a strained, hostile air about them as they stole furtive glances in our direction. For our part we rather enjoyed it. We knew their fun wouldn't last long. Sooner or later these fat young men would pay for the peaceful idleness they had enjoyed while the rest of their generation, all over the world, was fighting.

Suddenly there was a noise at the curtained entrance.

"Stoi!" said a Russian voice.

A young Russian cavalry officer dramatically flung aside the curtain and paused to survey the scene.

He was neatly turned out in dress uniform with a high choke collar and a tight fitting tunic covered with jangling medals. On his shoulders were the standard broad epaulets Stalin had recently resurrected from the Czarist Army. His blue breeches stood out at the hips with a flair any cavalry-man would be proud of. His high black leather boots were polished till they looked like patent leather. On an otherwise clean shaven, rather swarthy face the officer sported a pair of long bristling mustaches. On his head he wore a regulation Russian peaked cap set at an angle that alone would have proven he was a cavalryman.

But the main attraction was his sword. Although he was tall himself, the weapon hanging on his belt almost touched the ground. It was an ornate affair with a scabbard decorated with gold filigree. The hilt too was of gold and from it hung a thick gilt tassel. No doubt he'd "liberated" the monstrous curio from some palace or museum along the long road from Stalingrad.

For a moment we thought it was some sort of vaudeville act, but then the officer's orderly appeared in G.I. Russian uniform—so dirty, ill-fitting and tattered that no one could have imitated it. The officer glanced up and down the room till he caught sight of our uniforms. With a stiff parade-ground air he marched over to us, saluted, bowed, and stuck out his hand, "Lieutenant Mikhail Antonovich Chavadze, Third Guard Cavalry Division." We introduced ourselves. He removed his cap, passed it to his orderly whom he gruffly ordered to stand behind him, and sat down.

"Well, Comrade Allies," he began, rubbing his hands glee-fully, "this is a most pleasant surprise." He looked at my insignia. "And if I'm not mistaken, a fellow cavalryman! A double pleasure!" He paused and looked around. "But what should we drink?" He looked at our beer. "Bah, lousy stuff for a cavalryman. Shame on you!" He turned to his orderly. "Drag over one of those waiters, quick!"

Meantime the restaurant had come to a dead stop as though seized with a strange paralysis. The band had ceased playing. The golden youth had stopped dancing. The waiters stood motionless wherever they had been when the appari-tion burst through the curtains.

MacLean and I were a bit overwhelmed ourselves. The officer had hardly given us a chance to say a word. On the contrary, he had given every indication that for the time be-ing he was going to do the talking and get things organized so that we could have a really nice cozy inter-allied drinking bout.

A waiter was shaken out of his trance by the orderly and dragged before the dazzling cavalryman.

"Slivovitz, a bottle and three glasses," he commanded qui-etly but firmly. The waiter hesitated. It was the custom to pay before being served, he explained in an unsteady, obse-quious voice. I reached for some money in my pocket, hop-ing to avoid a messy scene. But the officer put his hand on my arm and said politely, 'Oh, no. This is my party—the

Red Army's party." He paused as the waiter hesitated. Then he looked at the waiter.

"Did you hear me? I said this is the Red Army's party." He spoke in a low deliberate voice, emphasizing each word. The waiter still hesitated. "I repeat, the Red Army's party." He put his right hand on the hilt of his sword and he gave the waiter a look that removed any last doubts as to what was going to happen next if he didn't get going.

A moment later a bottle of slivovitz appeared on the table. We each gulped down a glass. The cavalryman let out his breath with a roar, wiped his flowing black mustache on his sleeve and examined the scene about him. Something apparently was missing. He turned to his orderly and roared, "Music."

Before the orderly could act, the band suddenly woke from its death-like sleep and started playing.

The Lieutenant poured another round of slivovitz and another and several more. We were finally invited into the conversation and before long were swopping experiences in standard form.

The Lieutenant looked around the room again. Evidently something didn't please him. The golden youth were sitting silent at their tables, from time to time glancing moodily at us. The Lieutenant stood up and turned to them.

"Dance!" he commanded.

The golden youth looked up, stared at one another and fidgetted.

"Dance, I tell you," the Lieutenant bellowed.

A half-dozen couples rose uncertainly from their tables, shuffled to the dance floor and began to foxtrot though not with the gaiety they had displayed earlier. But still they danced.

We went on with our drinking and anecdote swopping. The Lieutenant was from the Caucasus, he told us. Had been in the army since the war. Enjoyed it immensely and really didn't know what he'd do when it was all over. He'd had a minor job in an office in Tiflis before. But after all the excitement he'd seen in the last four years he could never be satisfied with that again. His ancestors had all been fighters—it must be in his blood. He came from a real family.

" 'Khans' they called us, or 'princes.' Not like these Russian boors."

He cocked his thumb at his orderly standing at attention behind him. The orderly acknowledged the insult with a respectful bow.

Meantime the band had been playing and the golden youth dancing for over half an hour. Cautiously the band leader peered at the Lieutenant, but the latter was deep in the story of his life. Very quiety the music faded, and then died away, as though trying to tiptoe out of the Georgian's presence. The dancers, sweating like horses, stole back to their chairs.

"Georgia," the Lieutenant was saying, "that's a wonderful place. Wonderful women. Horses. Shooting. Everything. Music." Suddenly he became aware that the band had stopped. He whirled around in his chair and fixed a ferocious eye on the bandleader. The bandleader squirmed and tried to look away. The Lieutenant got up and marched across the dance floor. The bandleader bowed uneasily. .

"What Georgian songs do you know?" the Lieutenant demanded.

"I'm afraid we don't know any yet. But by tomorrow . . ."

"No Georgian music at all? And you call yourselves musicians. Uncultured, that's what you are, just plain uncultured. What Russian music do you know?"

" 'Black Eyes'," the bandleader suggested a trifle bashfully. " 'Black Eyes' is about all we've been allowed to play since the Germans came."

"All right," the Lieutenant sighed. "If that's all you know, play it." He put his hand on the hilt of his enormous sword. "And play it loud."

As he sat down again the band struck up "Black Eyes" with almost hysterical vigor. The Georgian resumed his story.

"I don't remember anything about the old days before the Revolution. I was much too young. Perhaps it's just as well." He gave a big wink and smiled mischievously. "From what my father told me before they arrested him, it must have been a pretty good life. But what the hell, I'm having plenty of fun."

Twenty minutes later the band was still playing "Black Eyes" and the golden youth, their last fling ruined, began to slip away.

Suddenly the Lieutenant paused. "But my goodness, they've not played a tune for you. How thoughtless of me!" He hurried over to the bandleader, called halt to "Black Eyes" and asked if they knew the Anglo-American national hymn. They didn't, the bandleader said, but they did know "It's a Long Way to Tipperary."

"Well, play that, then, and make it loud."

"Tipperary" went on and on until even the Lieutenant couldn't stand it. He turned to his orderly. "Tell that fat-headed bandleader I didn't intend him to play that tune till domesday—just enough to honor our honored guests." He bowed to us. "Tell him to play something else, anything he wants. If I want 'Black Eyes' or 'Tipperary' again, I'll let him know."

At last the second bottle of slivovitz was empty and we staggered to our feet.

"This is a good joint," the Lieutenant chortled happily. "Let's meet here again tomorrow afternoon." As he started for the door he clapped his hand on his sword and we marched out to the tune of "Black Eyes." When we got to the door, the cavalryman once more seized the hilt. The strains of "Tipperary" followed us up the stairs and through the passages to the street.

We never saw our Lieutenant again. For one thing the Russian Tsar was closed the next day by order of Tito. Soon afterward Belgrade's golden youth were mobilized into "voluntary" work squads to remove the rubble from the streets. Their well-cut suits and high-heeled shoes seemed a little incongruous in the heaps of broken brick and plaster and rubbish.

governments, grey beard,

and agreements

.

in

the woods battledress had been chic, except in the
Russian Military Mission where they always wore their dress
uniforms. But once we came to Belgrade, things began to
change. Fitzroy MacLean sent for his kilt and the attachments
that go with it. I sent for my breeches and Peel boots and a
long dress overcoat. But someone with a kind heart and a weak
head tried to send me a bottle of whiskey stuffed in the leg
of one of my boots. The bottle broke and my prize boots
acquired an odd shaped stain which no amount of polishing
ever got rid of.

Tito and his Partisans also began to put on the dog. At
first the Marshal took a villa on Rumianstev Drive, the most
fashionable residential street of Belgrade. But later he de-

cided to open up the White Palace of the ex-regent Prince Paul. King Peter's Royal Palace had been pretty badly battered in the fighting and, besides, architecturally it wasn't in the same class with the White Palace. Prince Paul, whatever his qualifications as regent, was an outstanding art collector, and the White Palace had at one time housed a collection of paintings second to none in the Balkans. Most of these had disappeared during the German occupation; it was generally assumed Hermann Goering had got his sticky hands on the best of them.

Even without the masterpieces, Tito and his staff managed to fix up the White Palace very regally with fine Persian carpets, some Aubusson tapestry, heavy flat silver and even the livery of the Prince's old staff. However, the embroidered insignia on the lapels of the livery had a few too many crowns for Tito's republican tastes. So the insignia had been removed, leaving a dark spot against the slightly faded blue of the rest of the uniform.

A few days after Tito had been installed, several of us went to lunch with him. He was an excellent host, very hospitable, informal and jolly, when he wanted to be. His secretary, Olga Ninchich-Humo, the daughter of an ex-Foreign Minister, who'd married a Moslem Communist from Sarajevo, had seen to it that the household staff was whipped into first rate shape. A good cook had been found, though not as good as Stepan who worked for me and whom Olga was constantly trying to kidnap. There were not more than ten or twelve for lunch including Tito, his Chief of Cabinet, Bakic, his then "Foreign Minister," Smodlaka, MacLean, and, if I'm not mistaken, a couple of visiting generals from AFHQ.

The chief topic of conversation was the negotiations between Tito and King Peter's Foreign Minister, Subasic, which were to determine what, if any, prerogatives and rights the King was going to keep in Yugoslavia. Tito argued that anything the King owned as an individual person was his to do what he liked with, but anything he enjoyed as King was for the "people" to dispose of. Tito was not too precise about who "the people" were, but we gathered he had a lot to do with them. Toward the end of the meal, Tito turned to me.

"I hear you went shooting last Sunday?" (In those days in Belgrade everyone knew what everyone else was doing, and not necessarily because of the Secret Police, which was only just getting organized.)

I said I had.

"Had pretty good luck, I'm told?"

"Yes, we bagged about fifteen pheasant and twenty hares," I answered. "Incidentally, I hear you were shooting too on Sunday, Marshal?"

"Yes, I went out."

"I'm told you had bad luck though. What did you get?"

"Not a damn thing," Tito answered.

"Then I suggest next time you're free you let me know. I can show you the best shooting in Serbia."

"Oh!" said Tito laughing. "And where do you usually go?"

"To the King's old shoot," I answered.

"The King's shoot?" Tito replied with a broad mischievous grin. He shook his finger admonishingly. "That's not for me! Tito never takes anything that belongs to the King." And he looked down modestly at his plate decorated with the royal coat of arms.

After lunch Tito said he wanted to show us a deep state secret he'd just discovered. With an air of great mystery he led us to the basement of the Palace, through a series of storerooms to a heavy iron door. He unlocked the door and swung it open dramatically. Then he turned a light switch and a long narrow vaulted passage appeared before us, descending gradually from the level of the door. We walked down the passage about fifty yards and came to another iron door, like a bulkhead. Tito unlocked this, turned some more switches and another stretch of corridor was lit up. A strange humming filled the tunnel. "Air conditioning," Tito explained smiling. "Old Paul did things up in style." Several smaller doors opened off the main corridor. Tito opened one and led us into a storeroom. On the shelves were row after row of flat black leather boxes. Tito opened one and took out a heavily ornamented gold fork.

"Real gold," he explained. "If you don't believe it, bite it."

He took us into another storeroom piled high with paintings.

"The missing paintings," he explained, "or at least some of them. I've asked the Belgrade Museum curator to come up and check them. Then we'll see how many the Germans got away with."

He picked up one small painting and examined it. A brass plaque identified it as a Rembrandt.

"I'm afraid I'm not much of an expert in these matters. My work up to now never gave me much time to study art." Behind the semi-sarcasm I thought I could detect a note of wistfulness. "It doesn't look as if I'll have much time to take up art for quite a while, either," Tito concluded with a laugh.

We went back out into the corridor and through another side door. It led into a small living apartment. There was a sitting room, a bedroom, a small bath.

"The Prince's air raid shelter," Tito explained. "Air conditioning, running water, electricity, and all two hundred feet underground. Not bad."

We followed the corridor down a gradual slope through several more bulkheads, perhaps a distance of five hundred yards, to another big iron vault door.

"We're now down in the valley behind the Palace," Tito explained. "That door opens out onto a small siding by the railroad tracks. I'm having it blocked up from the outside,"

he added, "since I don't expect to be using it myself," and he
laughed again.

Aside from getting his personal household set up, one of
Tito's problems after the capture of Belgrade was training
his guerrilla followers to act like well-trained government officials. For better or worse, he'd fired practically every civil
servant in Belgrade and now he had to replace them with his
own Partisans. It wasn't an easy job. It's not only a question
of finding people who know where the city gas supply turns
on or where the water mains run. Every government department has its own little power lines and gas mains, its files
and procedures developed over decades. The junior official
who doesn't decide things, but simply knows where the documents are, is sometimes highly underrated till he's fired.

One small side of the problem was protocol. Tito, himself,
I think fully understood the importance of protocol, diplomatic good manners, in his dealings with foreigners. In fact
he may even have overrated it. It is a common fault among
newcomers to high places. He probably figured, too, that
his plans required giving enough offense intentionally, without making extra trouble by insulting people unintention-
ally. But here again his awkward guerrillas were hardly the
brightest pupils of Emily Post. Time and again I heard Tito
upbraid them for some accidental discourtesy. I daresay some
of his upbraiding was more for the effect on the offended
than on the offender. But that was normal under the circumstances.

One cold winter evening I was working in my office when
the code clerk brought in an urgent flash from Airforce
Headquarters. Due to bad weather, it said, a bomber flight
had apparently attacked the wrong target somewhere in
Bosnia and had raised considerable havoc with a Partisan column, killing, among others, one of Tito's best generals. Since

Tito would probably protest, the Airforce wanted to let me know in advance so that I could register the necessary regrets, if and when called upon.

It was bad news for me, as I'd recently been having a rough time trying to work out several agreements with Tito, and I knew the incident wouldn't make him any easier to deal with.

A few minutes later, the phone rang. It was Olga, Tito's secretary.

The Marshal wanted to see me at once.

This is it, I said to myself, and I told Olga I'd be up at the Palace in fifteen minutes.

I bundled myself into my open jeep and drove the mile or two to the Palace gate through a cold bitter wind. The gates to the Palace grounds had previously always been open, but tonight they were shut and a Partisan guard, his tommy-gun at "port arms," blocked my way. I called to him that I'd been sent for by Tito and asked him please to open the gate.

The guard came over and firmly but politely told me that a new regulation required everyone to go through the back entrance. Had I had the slightest desire to see Tito that night, I'd have gladly gone in through a coal chute. But the shoe, fortunately, was on the other foot.

"But the Marshal sent for me," I persisted.

The guard obviously had his orders and no persistence or argument was going to move him.

"All right," I said after a few minutes. "Please send word to the Marshal that I called, but was turned away from the front gate and went home."

I turned the jeep around and drove home through the cold and snow.

I'd been back about half an hour when Olga called again.

"Where in heaven's name are you? The Marshal's raging at being kept waiting," Olga said.

"Didn't you get my message? I was stopped at the gate and told to go around to the servant's entrance. I told the sentry to tell you I was going home."

"Oh for God's sake, Charlie," Olga protested. "Don't be a child. There's a new security regulation that no one, not even cabinet ministers, can come in the front gate any more. Get off your high horse." Olga was always direct.

"As the representative of the United States in Yugoslavia, I have no intention of being treated like the baker's boy and told to come around to the back gate. I don't care what cabinet ministers do, I refuse to be sent through the servant's entrance."

Olga argued. I argued. In the end she hung up in disgust.

Ten minutes went by and Olga rang back. "All right, silly," she said. "I've arranged with the Captain of the Guard to have the front gate opened for you. Now for goodness sake, hurry! Tito's in a fury."

So back I went up the snowy cold road, wondering whether my little maneuver was going to work or backfire badly. The Palace gate was open wide as I drove up and the snow-covered guard grinned good naturedly as he saluted me. I was ushered through the numerous cordons of security guards that surrounded the Marshal and eventually shown into his study.

"Where have you been?" he began sternly. "I asked you to come over an hour ago."

"I'm sorry, Marshal," I replied, "but I suppose they told you what happened?"

"No, no one told me anything. People never tell me anything any more."

"Well, I came up as soon as you asked me and was stopped

by your own sentries at the front gate. I told them who I was and that you'd asked me to come up, but they said they had orders that I was to come in by the servants' entrance. So I turned around and went home."

Tito looked a little exasperated. "By the servants' entrance? What are they up to?" He sighed and sat back in his chair. "Really, the trouble those fellows have given me since we came to Belgrade! They just don't understand we're not still in the woods. They *can't* understand they're in Belgrade. To ask a foreign representative to come in by the back gate . . . Really! What can one do! And yet they're such wonderful fellows. But, then, what can you except in times like these?"

For ten minutes, he poured forth his troubles. At length he indicated he had nothing more to say, and I rose to go. When I reached the door I turned:

"But Marshal you sent for me to . . ."

"Oh yes! It's that bombing business up in Bosnia. Really, that was a tragic blunder and I'm most upset about it. Will you please tell General Eaker . . ."

"I've already had a message from the General saying how sorry he is about the mistake."

"I'm sure he is. Tell him I understand. In times like these, what can you expect?"

In the woods and in the early days after the capture of Belgrade, the Military Missions drew their daily supplies from Tito's Headquarters Commissariat. Everyone shared fairly in what was available. If you needed something extra and you knew where it could be got, you told the Commissariat which would go and get it. It was a good system and seemed to work out to everyone's satisfaction—no PX cards, no Commissary accounts, no Class Six Store rations. When there was wine or slivovitz to be had, each got his share. When there

wasn't any, you went dry. Unfortunately, the latter condi-
tion was the most common after we met up with the Red
Army. They had successfully drained the countryside of all
the wine and spirits that couldn't be hidden from their sharp
and inquisitive searches. So we were all keenly on the look-
out for new supplies.

About this time, I was taking an afternoon walk alone one
afternoon along the banks of the Danube. My walk was
partly for exercise, partly business. The Russians had announced, with a great deal of fanfare, that they'd just "given
a present" of fifty thousand tons of Russian wheat to starving
Belgrade, and that it had already arrived by Danube barge.
The gift was ballyhooed loudly in the Communist press and
by sly inferences it was made clear that the rich capitalist
countries like the United States, which were in a far better
position to supply food than poor war-torn Russia, were doing damn little to help the starving Yugoslavs. The population didn't react too elatedly to this gift until the amount was
inexplicably multiplied by ten in the press. The Russians
were sending not 50,000 tons but 500,000 tons.

Slavs are notoriously weak on the decimal system. 5,000,
50,000, 500,000 are used almost interchangeably to indicate
"lots." That is one of the reasons it's so difficult to analyze
Russia's Five Year Plans. You can never be sure that the
decimal point hasn't accidentally slipped over a digit or two.
I remember a Pole describing the death rate in a Soviet
prison camp he'd been in.

"There were 5,000 of us," he said, "and for a month the
death rate was over 1,000 a day."

So when the 50,000 tons of wheat suddenly shifted to 500,-
000, I wasn't too surprised. I was only curious to find out
where the decimal point really belonged.

We made some casual inquiries among the bargemen and
stevedores. Had they seen the fabulous wheat? Several of

them recalled that some barges of wheat had recently come *down* the Danube. They couldn't say exactly, but it might have been as much as 50,000 tons. No matter how you figured it, Russia was not *up* the Danube from Yugoslavia—at least not yet. Besides the Danube was blocked by wrecked bridges not far north of Belgrade.

Eventually we found out what had actually happened. The Germans, before they quit Belgrade, had requisitioned all the wheat they could lay hands on, loaded it on barges and started it up the Danube. But the barges didn't get very far before they were blocked by the bridges we'd bombed. Eventually they were overtaken by the Red Army and returned to the Yugoslavs. I suppose that when the Bolsheviks return stolen goods to their rightful owners, it is a gift. It is also very unusual.

Walking along the river front that day I didn't come across any wheat barges. But I did catch a glimpse of one of those tall, thin bottles the Germans put Rhine and Moselle wine in. The wine bottle was empty but the "Riesling" label was comparatively fresh and unsoiled. This was obviously worth investigating. I forgot about the mysterious wheat and started poking about a bit.

Soon I found a big storage depot nearby, surrounded by a high wooden fence with strands of barbed wire running along the top—just the sort of place the Germans would build to store their liquor. Inside the yard, I discovered case upon case of wine bottles, all neatly stacked in rows. There was champagne, French and German, Rhine Wine, Moselle, Burgundy and even Port. It would be just like the Germans, I thought, to booby-trap their liquor depots, so I cautiously approached the cases and peered at the bottles. The labels were intact. The corks although not sealed—after all, in wartime you can't have all the trimmings—were tightly rammed in. The cases themselves looked as if they had never been opened. I was tempted to break open a case and take out just one bottle. But my fear of mines got the better of me. After all, we could easily get a Partisan mine detector outfit to decontaminate the place and thus avoid the risk of blowing up the precious wine and myself.

I hurried home to the Balkan Hotel where I found Freddy Cole of the British Mission, who was now our Allied Supply Officer in addition to his other duties.

I told Freddy what I'd found.

I went back to my office to work but Freddy lost no time getting into action. Rounding up a couple of his officers and men, he jumped into a jeep and hurried off to find Tito's Chief of Commissariat. He told the latter about the cache and offered to lead him to it, provided the Partisans furnished a mine detector squad and a truck. The Commissariat Chief jumped into action and immediately produced a truck and a detector squad.

Toward evening I was hard at work in my office when the door flew open and three irate British officers stormed in.

"Trying to make fools of us, were you? Trying to make us look silly in front of the Partisans, eh?" They stood over me belligerently. "That wine cache . . . We spent two hours working with the Partisan mine detectors, and when we finally began to move the stuff onto the trucks, we discovered that every last bottle was empty!"

Along with the liquor situation the food and housing situation was beginning to deteriorate seriously from the standard we'd set in Valjevo. For some time, as the staff of the Mission grew, our quarters at the Balkan Hotel had been getting overcrowded. Besides, our Russian neighbors upstairs were beginning to monopolize not only working hours, which wasn't too serious, but my sleeping hours as well which was very serious indeed. So I began looking around for a building where we could house our whole staff and provide some sleeping space for the visiting generals who were beginning to plague us.

Most of the good houses had been grabbed by the Russians as soon as they reached Belgrade. And when they began to move north they didn't seem to be in much of a hurry to turn the houses free. Instead, they just expanded individually from corners of rooms to rooms, to apartments and finally to whole houses. You couldn't exactly blame them for in the Workers' Paradise they'd probably never had an apartment to themselves. There was little their Partisan hosts could do about it without being accused of inhospitality by the Kremlin. And it was at least three years too early for that. So, as usual when I was in difficulties, I went to my colleague, General Kisiliev, the head of the Russian Military Mission.

He was very helpful, and together we soon found an apartment house at the head of Belgrade's main street, which was being used as a Russian Army clinic. Kisiliev persuaded the clinic it could find smaller quarters and arranged to turn it over to us.

The building had had some rough treatment, first in the fighting and then in the "occupation." On the façade, for instance, you could make out the silhouettes of five German soldiers who'd been smashed against the walls by the explosion of a big shell right in front of the house. We couldn't clean off their remains but a coat of paint obliterated all but the most obvious traces.

Inside, things were even worse. The house had had several bathrooms, but apparently the first Russian troops to occupy it had found the intricacies of western plumbing too complicated for them and had ripped out everything but the faucets in the wall, leaving only the holes where the disposal pipes of the toilets went into the floor. Thus simplified, the bathrooms had served their new occupants well, though with considerable loss in sanitation. The clinic too had added its share of filth by the carefree manner in which it disposed of the blood and droppings of its customers. Our Mission doctor, Captain Bulinski, took one look at it and declared it unfit for human habitation. But it was the only house we could get and I decided to try to clean it up.

For six days a squad of "voluntary" workers shoveled and scrubbed until even Bulinski was satisfied. We found the discarded tubs, basins and toilets in the yard and put them back in place. Then we painted the house from top to bottom and moved in. Until I left, it was the headquarters of the Mission, and today it is used to house the women employees of the American Embassy, a monument to that fleeting phenomenon, Russo-American cooperation.

When I recall Kisiliev's helpfulness, I sometimes wonder whether he didn't read his mail from Moscow, or wheher, by his demonstrative collaboration with the Americans, he wasn't showing his little Yugoslav brothers that they were still just a second rate, uncultured small nation not fit to associate on equal terms with the big boys like Russia and America. Kisiliev, for all his charm and friendliness, was never a subtle politician. I hope he has survived somehow.

All during this period Yugoslavia was enjoying the luxury of two governments—King Peter's legal Government in London and Tito's rather more practical Government in Belgrade. A sort of interim working arrangement had been made in the summer of 1944 between Tito and Peter's Foreign Minister, Subasic. But now a more permanent arrangement was necessary. Negotiations for a more complete marriage went on for weeks between Tito, now installed in the White Palace, and Subasic who occupied a two-room suite in the Hotel Majestic. Fortunately I had strict instructions from Washington under no circumstances to get into the ring but to report the bout blow by blow.

The difficulties were innumerable. Was the new regime to be a constitutional monarchy or a republic? It was decided to leave that to "the will of the people." In the meantime, who would represent the head of state? It was decided to appoint three regents. Who were the regents to be? How many seats was each side, Tito's and the King's, going to have in the cabinet? Eventually, Subasic agreed to six seats against fifteen of Tito's and seven "others."

From then on things moved fairly fast. The new regents were sworn in at a double ceremony—Catholic and Ortho-dox—in Belgrade's Parliament Building. The Chiefs of the Three Allied Military Missions were asked to witness the event.

Metropolitan Josef, the Acting Patriarch, in full orthodox regalia celebrated the swearing in according to the rites of the Orthodox Church. He performed his functions before a small temporary altar covered with ikons, crosses and candles. Beside it, at another temporary altar, stood the Catholic Cardinal Bishop of Belgrade in his scarlet robes.

I couldn't help feeling that the whole affair was a little incongruous. Subasic, a devout Catholic, observed the ceremony reverently. Tito's henchmen all stood by stolidly. To all appearances they were as solemn as anyone present, but one couldn't escape the suspicion that at any moment they might start laughing.

I was glad when the ceremony was over and we went out of the sombre building. Things seemed a little more real in the bright sunlight. The participants all hurried away, Tito in a big shiny Packard, the rest in cars that had been resurrected from the garages of Belgrade's has-beens. I was one of the last to go. As I climbed behind the wheel of my jeep, the Catholic Bishop came up to me apologetically.

"You couldn't give me a lift, could you? I'm afraid there's no transportation for me."

He sat down in the low seat beside me and we drove off, his magnificent scarlet splendor contrasting sharply with the dirty little jeep. The incident, I thought, didn't augur too well for the Bishop's future. But then there had been something peculiar about the whole affair.

About this time, Tito was negotiating with Allied Headquarters in Caserta for civil aid to the Yugoslav population. These negotiations also dragged on for months, between a couple of delegates Tito had sent to Rome for the purpose and officers of AFHQ in Italy. I got the impression Tito's delegates were not all they might have been. Every time the subject of the negotiations came up between us, Tito would readily agree that the Allied demands were acceptable to him, but the next day his representatives in Rome would reject them. Eventually, slightly exasperated by the delay and the obvious incompetence of the Partisan delegates in Caserta, I sent a radio to Carmel Offie who was following the negotiations for the United States political advisor:

"Urgently suggest you send Allied negotiators to Belgrade to deal with the horse's mouth instead of wasting time at the other end."

The chief of communications in Caserta wired me to watch my language. (He apparently felt an obligation to keep the ether waves pure.)

But an Allied delegation eventually arrived in Belgrade under Generals Sadler and Hughes, and half an hour after conversations started with Tito, agreement had been reached. While the typists (Olga and my secretary, Sergeant Curly Laverdure) were making up the final drafts, we had lunch with Tito in the White Palace.

Then a hitch developed. Under the terms of the agreement, one of the London (Royal) members of the cabinet would have to countersign the agreement. The competent minister had just arrived from London the day before. I can't recall his name but we can call him Grey Beard for present purposes. Olga was told to call his hotel and get him up to the Palace before lunch. But he wasn't in his hotel and hadn't returned by the time we sat down to eat.

Olga was getting nervous and came asking for help. "What does he look like?"

Someone who knew him said he had a very long, grey beard. Olga called the Partisan Police.

"Please locate a gentleman who arrived yesterday from London with a very long, grey beard."

Lunch was over but no long, grey beard appeared. We sat about half an hour over coffee and still no beard. Tito took us on another tour of the secret underground escape corridor. When we came back upstairs not a trace of Grey Beard had been found. The generals from Caserta began to fidgit and look at their watches. If they were to get back to Italy by nightfall, there was not much time to lose. Eventually it was agreed they'd leave without the agreement and that it would be sent on as soon as the long, grey beard had countersigned it.

That evening at home I told some other members of the Mission about the trouble we'd had trying to find the Minister with the long, grey beard.

One of my companions began to laugh.

"That explains the excitement in town this afternoon," he said. "When I was walking down to the hotel around four, the main street was swarming with Secret Police. I asked a traffic cop what was up and he said he didn't know, but the rumor was they were arresting everyone with a grey beard."

Late that evening old grey beard himself tottered wearily home to his hotel, only to be pounced upon by a posse of policemen and secretaries flourishing the unsigned agreement. Without a murmur, he put his signature on the dotted line, and then mumbled apologetically that he'd just been out having tea with some old friends he hadn't seen in five years. "Can't a Cabinet member do even that in Belgrade?" he asked plaintively.

for

many months after the capture of Belgrade we were still, for all practical purposes, behind the enemy lines. Though we'd linked up with the Red Army, there were enough German troops between ourselves and our base to make it impossible to get in or out, except over the top. Eventually Saloniki was cleared and it was possible to travel overland to the Aegean and thence by sea to Italy around Greece. But it was a very long way round.

So the air route between Italy and Belgrade was our only practical line of communication, and Zemun, Belgrade's airport, from the first day of "liberation," took on a special importance. Zemun was the best airfield in the Balkans, with a long, broad, concrete runway. The hangars, control tower and all the technical installations had been thoroughly destroyed during the German retreat, but there was nothing wrong with the precious runway that a few bags of cement wouldn't fix.

For the first day or so after the airport was captured, Russian fighters needed it for close-up tactical air-support. But then the Germans retreated further and the Russians moved up to other fields. Tolbukhin must have realized it would be impossible to keep this prize field for himself, to the exclusion of the Partisans, the British and ourselves. And since the Red Airforce doesn't like sharing a field with allies, who might "spy" on their latest models of equipment or even observe their strange flying techniques, they preferred to pull out altogether, leaving only some air transport planes at Zemun. The latter were either lend lease DC-3's or Russian copies of DC-2's, so there was nothing much to arouse their allies' illegitimate curiosity.

We'd been pressing the Russians fairly hard for several days to let us use the field and there was a big backlog of planes waiting at various airbases in Italy to come in. In those days, German flak and fighter planes were still strong enough to make it unhealthy to fly over from Italy by daylight without fighter escort. As the Airforce had better use for its fighters than escorting a lot of OSS screwballs in and out of the Balkans, most of our flights were at night.

The first problem that arose when the Rusians quit using the field was, who was going to run it? The British had been training some Partisans in airfield operations in Egypt, but these were the first to admit they couldn't do it without help. The British said they'd run it. Not to be outdone, the Russians suggested they'd run it. Although I hadn't the vaguest idea about running airfields, I couldn't let our side down, so I offered to run it. It was finally agreed we'd all run it together.

Operating an airfield by a quadripartite committee was not, it developed, an ideal solution. The British and ourselves had more or less similar systems for bringing our planes in, the Russians had an entirely different system, and the Partisans had not had time as yet to develop any system at all; they just brought their few planes in by hand.

Then there was the question of who decided whose planes were coming in at what times, and who got the landing lights operating so they'd only be on the few seconds it took to bring a plane down without giving some stray German Stuka a chance to have some fun.

There was then no particular friction over the airport and everyone was anxious to do his share and cooperate. The result, however, was confusion—thorough, hair-raising confusion. It started with a bang the first night the quadripartite scheme went into effect. The British announced there'd be six planes in from Italy at 2300 hours.

"That's interesting," said the Russian Airforce Colonel. "We have eleven planes coming in at 2315."

It was already nine p.m. so there was not a chance of changing the arrivals. The British Wing Commander looked a little harassed.

"I have a sort of walky-talky machine here to talk to the pilots. Maybe I can keep my planes away until the Russians are on the ground." Then half to himself, he muttered, "But I've never known the damn machine to work yet."

Just to keep him on his toes, I reminded him that one of the six planes was bringing in twelve Allied journalists. "Of course, we want to give them a good show," I added.

The Wing Commander winced and walked off into the mud. It had been raining for days and, except for the concrete runways and approaches, the field was a vast swamp. A few minutes later he waded back, his boots caked with mud almost to the knees.

"We'll have to warn the pilots not to run off the concrete or they'll never get out of the mud. Don't suppose you've got a tractor here, in case one of them does get stuck?" the Commander asked a Partisan major, in impossible Serbian.

But the Partisan Major understood and said, "No."

The Wing Commander groaned and waded out into the mud again to compose his thoughts.

A British major turned a flashlight onto his watch.

"Thirty minutes till they're due."

The Commander sloshed back onto the concrete apron in front of the wrecked control tower.

"You have tested the landing lights, haven't you, Major Kerkich?" he asked the senior Partisan present.

"Runway lights?" the Major answered a little vaguely. "Why yes, I told Lieutenant Bakic to have them fixed this afternoon. Let's see if they work."

He opened a box hidden in the ruins of the control tower and flipped a switch. We looked out onto the runway. It was black as pitch. He flipped it again. Nothing happened. He looked rather hurt and puzzled.

"Can't think why Lieutenant Bakic didn't put them into shape."

Now, even the Russian Colonel roused himself out of his placid calm.

"No runway lights? Good God, man, how are the pilots going to know where to land? Have you any flares? Quick, some flares. Idiot!"

"I haven't any flares," the harassed Partisan replied, stung by the Russian Colonel's insult. "What about some tin cans though? I saw a bunch of cans back in the junk heap behind the hangar this afternoon. We could fill them with gasoline. They'd show up on a night like this."

No one had any other suggestion, so we all scurried over to the dump heap and began grubbing around with flashlights looking for tin cans. We dumped them into the jeeps and someone dashed off for a jerry can of gas. Back and forth up the runway the jeeps scurried, spacing the tin cans and filling them with gas. Finally a few moments before 2300 we lit them.

"They're a bit dim," said the Wing Commander. "Let's hope the pilots have good night eyes. We could put one jeep at the head of the runway and flash its headlights down it to show them which way to come in."

"Let's use your jeep, Commander," the Russian Colonel suggested with a grin.

A moment later there was a faint purr of engines in the air above us.

The Commander strapped his "machine" across his ample middle, began to crank it and scream into a microphone.

"Hello B-618, this is C-214. Do you hear me, over?"

There was a pause and silence. He cranked again.

"Hello, B-618, this is C-214, do you hear me, over?"

Silence. A muffled curse from the Commander. The planes were beginning to circle. The Commander kept on cranking and shouting impatiently, "Can you hear me, over?"

As the sound of engines came closer, he tore the machine off his chest and tossed it far out into the mud. He pulled out a Verey pistol and called to the Russian. "Are those your planes?"

"Damned if I know," the Colonel replied quietly.

"Well, how can you get them to identify themselves?"

"Can't," said the Colonel. "It's forbidden."

"Then what are we going to do?"

"Just let them land. They'll do all right." The Colonel wasn't going to get excited if he didn't have to.

"But suppose they're our planes. They won't land till I signal them with Verey lights," the Commander explained. "I can't let 'em stay up all night."

"Then signal them to come down. What's your signal for that?" the Russian said.

"Two greens and a red."

"Two greens and a red? Hell, that's our signal to go away!" the Russian protested.

The Commander already had his pistol raised, about to fire the flares into the air. He lowered his arm and in utter despair said, "All right, now what the hell do we do?" The drone of the engines was so loud you could hardly hear him.

A glaring light suddenly appeared just behind the jeep at the end of the runway, illuminating the whole group of us standing in the middle of the concrete.

"Good God, they're coming in to land," someone yelled and we scattered to the sides. The plane's landing lights caught the jeep just as the pilot was bringing his wheels down to the ground. The engines raced, the plane gave a little hop, popped over the jeep and settled down on the strip. As he flashed by we could see the Red Army star on the fuselage.

"Well, thank God, the Russians are here first. Once they are out, it'll be easy." The Wing Commander momentarily looked relieved.

The Russian Colonel took over, which consisted chiefly of lighting a cigarette and counting the planes as they popped over the jeep, like sheep over the fence. If there were enough planes, I thought, the Colonel would probably go to sleep.

Almost all the Russian planes had come in. Several were already unloaded and were taxiing up the approach to the runway ready to take off again. But the air was still full of the drone of engines.

Suddenly a series of lights shot out from one of the planes in the air.

The Colonel looked up at the signal. "Means nothing to me. Must be your chickens, Commander."

The Commander loaded his Verey pistol and shot another series of lights in the air.

"What did you tell 'em?" the Colonel asked curiously.

"To get the hell out of here for a while."

"Excellent advice, I'd say," said the Colonel, as the last of his eleven monsters popped over the jeep onto the runway. "I'll get my babies out of here as quickly as I can."

When the last of the Russian planes had taken off, the Wing Commander began firing off more Verey lights to call back his wandering planes. More Verey lights answered, and soon the first American plane came in for a landing, jumped the jeep at the end of the runway and put down gently on the concrete. The Wing Commander dashed down the runway in another jeep to lead the plane to the unloading apron. The plane swung around and dutifully followed the Wing Commander's jeep. As it closed up on the jeep, the Wing Commander sped ahead. But the pilot seemed afraid of being left alone, for he too stepped on the gas as though to grab at mummy's coattails. Soon jeep and plane were coming back down the runway hell for leather, the jeep going all out, the big '47 breathing right down the Wing Commander's neck like a greyhound after a hare.

About forty yards from the head of the runway, the Wing Commander couldn't stand it any longer. He cut the jeep sharp to the left off the runway into the mud. The jeep skidded, the tires screeched, and the Commander's Partisan assistant who was riding beside him promptly fell out onto the concrete. The pilot of the taxiing plane, however, was not going to be shaken off. He swung his plane sharply, his wheels just missing the dazed Partisan lying below him, and the plane headed off the runway after the jeep. The plane's big wheels hit the soft mud and promptly settled into it up to the hubs. The pilot gunned the engines, flapped his flaps, waggled his rudder, but only the propellers moved.

The plane was now nicely stuck with its tail half way across the runway. The dazed Partisan, unhurt but rather bewildered, picked himself up, dusted himself off, climbed back into the jeep and sat down to await the next excitement.

The Russian Colonel who was standing beside me accepted a cigarette. There was a slight smile on his face as I gave him a light with my Zippo. "Sometimes," he said, very quietly so no one else could overhear, "it's better to let the pilots do their own taxiing."

The Wing Commander walked over to the stranded plane.

You could almost see the blue line of invective he directed up at the window of the pilot's cabin.

As he ran out of breath, a thick Carolina accent came meekly from the cabin:

"But suh! Ah wasn' gwanna run yuh down, suh. Ah just didn' wanna get too fah behahn yuh, suh!"

A second plane was already coming in for a landing, unaware that the fine Zemun strip now looked more like the Grand National steeplechase course at Aintree than a runway. Someone parked a jeep with its headlights faintly illuminating the stranded C-47's tail which lay directly in the path of the incoming ship.

Throughout the whole harrowing evening, my own role had been purely honorary. The fine points of aviation had always been way over my head. But one thing I remembered reading in the papers was that when planes crack up, they often explode. As inconspicuously as possible I strolled off into the muddy morass of the airfield and didn't stop until I was beyond the range of flying debris. Then I sat down on a discarded box (the Wing Commander's machine it turned out), buried my face in my hands and waited.

The second plane was already gliding in for the landing. Its idling engines suddenly spurted. That was to get over the first jeep, I told myself, and braced for the crash. The engines slowed again for an instant and then picked up with a mighty roar. He'd seen that C-47's tail in front of him and was trying to jump it. I put my fingers in my ears, shut my eyes and ducked my head. For almost a full minute the roar continued. When I finally looked up, the plane, a vague shadow, was climbing back into the air. Apparently that second hurdle had been too much for the pilot and he had decided to go back up and think things over. I wondered how a judge at the Grand National would have ruled on that. Would he have called it a refusal if a horse didn't come back to earth after jumping the fence at Beecher's Brook?

For several minutes the plane circled, while the unfortunate pilot tried to figure out what those morons below were cooking up for him. Then he came in as slowly as his big load allowed. He passed well over the jeep, skimmed the tail of the mud-bound '47, hesitated a second as though to see whether we'd added a third hurdle and then, satisfied we had not, settled cautiously on the concrete beyond. Fortunately it was a good long runway and he was able to stop before he ran off the end. Then he taxied back to the start (this time no one volunteered to guide him) and parked in the lee of his mud-bound comrade.

Out of the plane spilled twelve English and American journalists. Some of them seemed a little shaken but, true to their profession, they weren't going to show it. While we waited for the rest of the planes, they huddled in little groups swopping experiences the Zemun landing had reminded them of.

"Once when we were landing in Tangiers on one engine. . . ."

"I recall hitting the Peking runway when both tires. . . ."

"I'll never forget taking off from Tehran once when the pilot retracted the landing gear before we were off the ground. . . ."

I wondered what they'd soon be saying about "the time I first came into Zemun."

The other four planes had been watching the circus from above and obviously suspected we had booby-trapped the field. One by one they slipped in cautiously, well above the jeep and their stranded colleague, and settled down comfortably beyond the hurdles. When they were all in, we set to work extricating the fellow in the mud. For an hour or two we dug, pulled, pushed, pried and sweated. At last the plane was back on solid concrete and before long they were all off again to Italy.

Three or four of the journalists rode back to town with me.

"I saw a couple of Russian officers out on the field. I suppose they were responsible for the mess?"

"No, can't say they had much to do with that operation," I answered cautiously.

"How badly are the Russians behaving in Belgrade, anyway?" another correspondent asked.

"They're most of them gone by now," I told them, "and it's not the same place without them."

MacLean and I had been urging Tito for some time to let a group of journalists visit Belgrade and see for themselves what was going on. It was far better, we argued, to get the whole truth publicized than the distorted rumors that were inevitable as long as Belgrade was shrouded in mystery. When the physical prerequisites, the beds, food and transportation were available, Tito finally agreed.

The correspondents were a mixed bag. Among them were some of the best foreign correspondents in the trade—and some of the worst. There had already been a few intrepid reporters in the woods before them, John Phillips of *Life* and Stoyan Pribichevitch of *Time*, among them. Pribichevitch, an American, came originally from a well known Serbian family and was on the scene when the other journalists arrived. In

fact, he was in my office the next morning when some of the
newly arrived Americans came in, ostensibly to ask a few
questions. Within a few minutes, the questions were forgotten and the more vociferous were well started on a bitter
battle (you could hardly call it an argument) pro and con
Tito, pro and con King Peter, pro and con Mikhailovitch.
Facts, fiction, rumor, history and myth were cited in angry
voices. A particularly buxom female correspondent—she must
have stood six foot three and was well proportioned—disagreed with something Pribichevitch said. The battle got hot-
ter and louder. When she had practically exhausted her invective, she walked over to Pribichevitch, grabbed him by the
lapels (Pribichevitch was a good foot smaller than she) and
shook him as though she were puffing up a pillow.

"Damn it," she said, "I wonder if you're even an American."

Exactly where that question fitted into the argument I
couldn't figure out, but Stoyan shook himself loose, straightened out his coat, stuck out his chest and answered:

"Madame, you forget I'm an American by choice, not by
accident."

But the journalists were only our first visitors. After them
came special missions, relief missions, typhus missions, junket-
ing officials and, of course, the visiting general.

Generals have a weakness for visiting their fellow generals
whenever the latter have just captured another city. Ostensibly the visit is to congratulate their colleagues. Usually it's
because the visiting general has a few days free for sightsee-
ing, or else his aides have just heard you can buy Leicas or
silver or Meissen China or caviar cheap in the newly liberated city.

The generals themselves didn't cause too much trouble. We
got them at the rate of about two a week—about the same

rate as we get Congressmen in peacetime. It was their staffs who made the fuss. Generals' staffs are the greatest antique collectors that ever bought a figurine. And they're not terribly particular about how antique something is. If it's a good buy they buy it. And what they don't do to the exchange rate is not worth talking about. All you had to do was fly a big silver plane with some stars on it over Belgrade and the dinar would rise ten points in the black market before the plane could land.

Fortunately both MacLean and I had heard what had happened in some of the previously liberated capitals. So almost our first telegram to AFHQ after the fall of the city said that a strict system of visas or clearances for Belgrade was being put into force. (We didn't say by whom, but we strongly, and not entirely accurately, implied by Tito himself.) The system forbade anyone entering Belgrade who did not have a clearance issued through one of the two Missions. The message may not have been the most ethical I ever sent, but I'm inclined to think it delayed for many months the Partisans' putting in a much stricter system of their own.

I was so impatient to get that message off before a flood of visitors arrived that I asked Bill Callanan to code it at ten o'clock one evening. Bill apparently had other fish to fry and protested vigorously.

"Hell," he said, "that can wait till tomorrow's radio contact. Coding cables is no way to spend an evening, particularly that silly kind of telegram."

I tried to explain why the message was important but Bill would have none of it. Besides he was to be transferred in a day or two and it was all the same to him whether Belgrade was subjected to a plague of locust colonels or not.

"But, Bill," I said, getting a little fed up. "I'll admit it's not much fun coding but that's true of lots of things in the army. Orders, after all, are orders in the army."

"Army?" said Bill, startled. "Did you say army? Hell, man, we're not in the army. We're in the OSS."

I coded the telegram myself.

Our clearance system worked out in the long run quite well, except for the generals and Tex McCrary. We never really expected it to work for generals and until then I had never run across Tex. The first time we got a radio flash that a general and his staff were on their way to Zemun without clearance, I sent a young lieutenant down to the field to tell the general when he arrived to go away. Then I sat back in my office and waited for the lieutenant's report. Unfortunately, the lieutenant didn't report but the general did. It was a rather stormy interview and we decided thereafter to consider generals—even brigadier generals—in a special category.

Tex McCrary flew his own way into the same category. One evening a day or so after we'd "liberated" Belgrade, I was dining with General Korneev. A Soviet Airforce colonel came up to me and said that they'd had quite a time with an American plane at Zemun the day before. I asked what had happened.

"Well," he said, "an American Airforce plane came swooping around Belgrade yesterday morning apparently taking pictures or something. You hadn't told us to expect anyone, so we sent up a few fighters to invite him down for a chat. At first he seemed a little suspicious of our invitation but we put on some heat and eventually he lowered his landing gear and came in. When we questioned him, it was obvious he was on a routine mission and had simply got his routine a little mixed up. We told him next time to check with you first. But the whole thing's taken care of now."

"But where is the plane? Where's the pilot?" I asked. "If he isn't back at base, they'll report him missing and there'll be hell to pay."

"Oh, don't worry. Everything's fixed up. I only told you because I thought you'd be amused."

So I forgot about it till the next morning, when a grimy unshaven Airforce colonel stumbled into my office, looking a little tired and bleary-eyed.

"My name's McCrary," the Colonel said and stuck out his hand. "You're Charlie Thayer?"

I admitted I was.

"Had an emergency landing two days ago on Zemun field. Russians have been entertaining or detaining me ever since, I don't quite know which."

"You weren't by any chance forced to land by the Russians, were you?"

"Well, in a manner of speaking, when they got on my tail I thought I'd better land. You see, I had a camera plane and it isn't as fast as some of their fighters."

I said the Russians had told me their side of the story and had promised me everything was in order. I had assumed he was safely home long ago. By this time he was undoubtedly on the missing list. Just what had happened?

"Well, you see, the Airforce wanted some pictures of all the destroyed bridges over the Danube. So I said I'd come and snap them. But the Russians seem a bit suspicious."

"But why didn't you ask for a clearance first?"

"Hell, I wasn't going to land, and besides I fly over Germany all the time and I don't ask *them* for clearance. Why should I ask the Russians? This is Yugoslavia, isn't it?"

There's a certain earthy logic about Airforce officers that it would be a pity to try to confuse with a lot of international law. So I merely suggested that in the future, if he'd make his travel arrangements through us, we might be able to facilitate his journeys.

As he left, Tex murmured something about the other bridges he still had to snap up Hungary-way.

"Have you clearance?" I asked.

Tex muttered a reply I couldn't make out, except that I knew it wasn't "Yes."

We had a message next day that Tex had returned late the previous evening—a suspiciously long time after he'd left us. I presume the Airforce got all its pictures.

among

our VIP visitors was General Leon
Fox of the Typhus Mission who was with us on and off for
months. His duty was to locate and, if possible, stop any
typhus epidemic that might get started as a result of the shortages, the disruption of sanitary services and, above all, the
mass migrations that a war invariably sets in motion. Fox
claimed that all the major epidemics of typhus that have swept
Europe, particularly after World War I, started somewhere
in the Balkans. If the mission could catch an epidemic in time,
or at least, if they could check it before it got out of the
Balkans, they might be able to prevent a repetition of the
slaughter typhus had caused in 1918-1919.

So the War Department gave General Fox a staff of doctors and biologists, planes, jeeps, and enough DDT to make the louse world tremble for its life. The Balkans was only one of Fox's trouble spots. Sometimes he'd dart off to India or Africa or Persia for a while, but he always ended up back with us in Belgrade.

Tito, when Fox had explained what he wanted to do, was enthusiastic and more or less gave him carte blanche to go ahead. Fox's mission scoured the country from one end to the other looking for typhus and lice. He tested. He inoculated. He dusted DDT powder, and in the end he pretty well succeeded not only in preventing a European epidemic but in stopping most of the minor epidemics in Yugoslavia. It was one of the rare battles we won before it had to be fought. It was not an easy job and not undangerous. Fox's doctors were forever dashing into newly captured towns to start their dusting and inoculating just as soon as the last shot had been fired and before the mine detectors had had a chance. As a result several were killed by enemy mines and booby traps.

But everyone has drawbacks. With Fox it was his white mice and guinea pigs.

Field Marshal Alexander, the Supreme Commander in the Mediterranean Theater, had decided to come to Belgrade to discuss with Tito the question of supplying his Partisans along the Adriatic Coast and coordinating operations when Allied troops joined up with the Partisans around Trieste. (The war ended before the "join up" and when they did finally make contact the problem was not how to fight together but how not to fight each other.)

I had invited Alexander to lunch with me in Belgrade when he arrived, and he had accepted. But the trouble with Field Marshals is that they don't operate on schedules like railroad trains. If we knew in advance when we wanted it, Corporal Mike Yovanovich, our master caterer and man of all trades, could "lay on," to use the phrase of the era, a

very fine meal. But we didn't know when Alexander was coming, and we didn't have an icebox. Mike rose to the situation
nobly and, instead of buying his food at the butchers, he
bought it in farmyards on the hoof. By the time Alexander
arrived, our diminutive backyard was a swarming menagerie
of lambs, chickens, geese and ducks. To make matters more
complicated, General Fox blew in the evening before on one
of his periodic visits, with a huge new stock of guinea pigs
and white mice.

The lunch started off well enough. As a special treat Mike,
who never should have wasted his time in the army, had "arranged" about five kilos of fresh black caviar from Rumania—
how, I never knew and never asked. Mike was just that kind of
an operator who could get the precious caviar four hundred
miles across Rumania, where there were few roads and fewer
bridges, without blinking an eye. Anyway, we had caviar,
sour cream and blini for a first course.

After that came a light consommé with croutons. I'd been
telling the Field Marshal some of the minor headaches of life
in Belgrade. I explained, as any housewife might, how difficult life was without an icebox, how we'd had to turn the
backyard into a farmyard to keep our food fresh. I even told
him of Fox's guinea pigs and white mice.

The Field Marshal winced. "You mean the white mice
were all mixed in with the food. . . ."

"Oh, no!" I said as convincingly as I could. "We kept the
white mice quite separate, I think."

At that moment a waiter passed a dish of cheese croutons.
They were little pink round things about as big as your
thumb and had four little protuberances, like legs, sticking
out of each pink ball.

The Field Marshal took one look at them, glanced at me
and said:

"You won't mind if I don't have any, will you?"

The rest of the meal passed off fairly well. It was hardly a light lunch that Mike had "laid on." After about four meat and vegetable courses, he produced an enormous dish of Moussaka.

The Field Marshal sat back wearily as he finished his plate, and sighed:

"Really, I do hope there's no more. I can't take it much longer."

"Oh, don't worry. That's all except for dessert. Usually they end with suckling pig. It's the tradition and our chef is a strong traditionalist. But today for the first time," I added very smugly, "I've finally managed to show him who's boss and simply ordered him to leave out the pig. It's sometimes hard to assert your authority with these Serbs. They take a lot of understanding. But this time I'm glad to say I succeeded, even if it was just with the cook."

As I finished my pompous little speech on how to command Serbs, the double doors of the pantry opened and the headwaiter marched proudly in holding an enormous platter in each hand above his head. Sitting prettily on each platter was a fat suckling pig.

Infinitely courteous as he always was, the Field Marshal turned to me:

"Colonel, is this your first command?"

That night Tito gave a reception for the Field Marshal. As usual I was a little late. When I walked into the backroom where Tito, Alexander and the other Mission Chiefs were, I noticed Tito turn and whisper something to a waiter. A moment later four glasses of slivovitz were served up to me.

"Colonel," Tito said, "you're the lowest ranking Mission Chief here and yet you're always the last to turn up. For a punishment, you can knock back those four glasses of slivovitz."

I argued that being on time fifty times a day for four years

at West Point had used up all the punctuality I'd ever had
in me. But Tito and Alexander were unconvinced, and I did
as I was told. As I finished the fourth glass, General Kisiliev
passed me a fifth. "And now, Colonel, I'd like to propose a
toast to the American Army, our great ally. Bottoms up."

But I couldn't take more than half the glass.

Kisiliev protested vehemently.

"What, you only drink half a glass to your own Army?"

"But, General," I sighed, "I thought you meant that half
of our Army which is fighting your German enemies. I can't
believe you're drinking to the half that's fighting your friends,
the Japs."

Tito turned to the Russian:

"That'll be a four glass fine for you, General."

Kisiliev took his punishment like a gentleman.

When he had recovered, Alexander asked him, "Where's
Marshal Tolbukhin? In Budapest?"

Kisiliev allowed as how he might be.

"I'd hoped very much to see him and discuss some rather
important matters, but I can't get any answer from him."

Kisiliev said he was sorry, but he didn't know why Tolbukhin didn't answer his mail. "Perhaps he's too busy," he
suggested airily.

With that charmingly mild tone typical of Alexander, he
replied:

"Yes, when you have to run an Army Group, you must be
busy. I can appreciate that from the way the Mediterranean
Theater with its several Army Groups keeps me busy. But
still I'd like to see Tolbukhin, and I'd be prepared to leave
my Theater for a day to visit him, if he can't leave his Army
Group."

Kisiliev got the point, said he'd see what he could do and
disappeared.

It was almost midnight before he returned. He was a little

breathless. There was a lot of whispering in corners for a few minutes and then it was announced that the Field Marshal would visit Tolbukhin at his Headquarters "in Hungary" the next day.

Ten bleary-eyed Englishmen and Americans clambered onto a Soviet C-47 at five o'clock the next morning and took off for "Hungary." Each time we asked the Russians where precisely in Hungary we were headed for, a vague dreamy look came into their eyes and they replied:

"Just Hungary. We're going to Hungary. It's a little country."

The Field Marshal was persistent.

"Please tell me, are we going to Budapest or not?" His voice was sterner than usual.

The Russians looked dreamier and vaguer than ever. "Sir, our orders are to take you to Marshal Tolbukhin's Headquarters. If that's Budapest, then we're going to Budapest. If it isn't, then we aren't going to Budapest."

Finally we gave up asking and relaxed.

An hour out of Belgrade—we could scarcely have crossed the Hungarian frontier—the engines slowed down and the plane dipped toward a landing. So it wasn't Budapest, for Budapest was at least an hour further on.

On the landing strip, we were met by a bevy of Soviet Generals and a dozen snappy looking civilian cars, mostly German Mercedes, and Horchs. We were quickly distributed into the cars, each with a General as escort, and set off across the country.

I asked the General in our car the sixty-four ruble question once more.

"Could you tell us, General, just where the Marshal Tolbukhin Headquarters are?"

"That's where we're going," he replied blandly.

"Yes, I understand that, but where geographically? Can you tell me the name of the town?"

"I'm afraid I can't. You know how hard these names around here are to pronounce, and I'd hate to misinform you."

"That airport we just came into, could you tell me its name?"

"I'm afraid I can't," the General replied. "It's the first time I was ever there."

"But is it in Yugoslavia or Hungary?"

"I'm afraid I don't know that either. Never was any good at Central European geography."

I stopped asking questions and began looking for clues along the road. We passed a roadsign the Germans and Russians had both forgotten to take down. It pointed to a tiny village off the main road called Kcmytcskt or something of the sort.

"If that name's any indication, we're in Hungary now," I commented.

"Are we?" said the Soviet General.

For an hour and a half we bounced over atrocious country roads. From the position of the sun, we were heading roughly northeast. The dust was appalling and, to avoid it, we fell well back from the cars ahead. We went through a village. As we came out of it, there wasn't a sign of the pillar of dust the cars ahead had been kicking up.

The General looked about the rolling countryside uneasily. He murmured something to the driver. At the next village crossroad, we stopped and the driver asked a villager a question in Hungarian. The villager waved us down a side road.

"Isn't it difficult to have to ask your way when you don't know where you're going?" I asked the General.

"Indeed it is," he answered, beaming affably at me.

My watch read nine o'clock when we finally came to the outskirts of another village, where we were halted by a Soviet sentry.

The sentry told us the rest of the party, including the Field Marshal, hadn't arrived yet. The General suggested we wait till they come before going on. Then he turned to me, smiling sweetly.

"Sometimes you make better time when you don't know where you're headed. 'The easier you take it, the further you go,' " he added, quoting a Russian proverb.

Ten minutes later a cloud of dust behind us indicated that the rest of the cavalcade had turned up and together we all proceeded into the village, and down the main street to a large peasant cottage surrounded by flowers and fruit trees.

"This," said the General, "is Marshal Tolbukhin's Headquarters."

Anything less like a Headquarters you could scarcely imagine. The village couldn't have had more than a hundred houses in it and all of them, with the exception of the Town Hall, were small peasant cottages. Except for a sentry or two along the street, there was not a soul to be seen. No automobiles, other than our own cavalcade, no telephone lines, messengers, motorcycles or any of the other paraphernalia you'd expect in the smallest command post, to say nothing of an Army Group Headquarters.

We were ushered into the cottage called "Tolbukhin's Headquarters." There was no one in the livingroom. A moment later Tolbukhin tramped in, unaccompanied, through the back door and introduced himself.

Of the many Russian Generals and Marshals I've seen, Tolbukhin came the closest to being what one imagines a Russian General ought to look like. He was tall, fat and round faced. Slightly bald, his hair was neatly combed straight across his high domed forehead down almost to his small blue eyes.

Everything about him indicated the mild, self-confident patri-
archal chief—kind when he wanted to be, ruthless when he
had to be. You could easily imagine him in a white Russian
peasant blouse pottering about his great country estate, the
"little father" of a thousand serfs.

"I suggest a light breakfast, gentlemen, before we settle
down to talk. You've come a long way and you probably need
a little refreshment." He made a gesture of emptying a vodka
glass and his eyes twinkled pleasantly.

"Vodka starting at 11:00 a.m.! It looks to me like another
hands-across-the-caviar conference," MacLean whispered to
me. "The Field Marshal won't get much change out of him, I
fear."

Tolbukhin lead us into a rather large diningroom. A T-
shaped table had already been laid with an elaborate assort-
ment of silver and glassware.

At the head of the table, Tolbukhin took his place with
Alexander on his right and General Lemnitzer, Alexander's
American deputy on his left. On Alexander's other side sat
Colonel General Zheltov, Tolbukhin's deputy. Zheltov, whom
I was going to see a lot of over the next months, was built
like a wrestler, with a thick bull neck, beedy eyes, a sly sour
smile on his puffy cheeks. As he later explained, he was the
Communist Party watchdog of Tolbukhin's Headquarters.

The rest of us distributed ourselves around the banquet
tables, MacLean and myself at the inner angles of the T
where we could easily interpret for our chiefs at the head of
the table.

Breakfast started with pickled herring, ham, sardines,
cheese and vodka. The usual toasts were drunk from substantial vodka glasses, constantly replenished by a squad of
uniformed Russian WAC's. I stole a glance at our Russian
hosts to see whether their vodka came from the same carafes
as ours did. Tolbukhin caught my eye just as one of the

WAC's was surreptitiously filling his glass from a different carafe than the one she used for Alexander.

"Young man," Tolbukhin said, "it seems to me you're about five ranks junior to almost everyone else at this table—about seven ranks below me at any rate. It ill-behoves you, therefore, to pry into my little weaknesses. The fine is three glasses of vodka."

Stuffing my mouth with as much butter as I could lay hands on, I swallowed it and then tossed back the vodka, hoping the grease would protect my much abused innards. It was a trick I had picked up in Moscow.

From then on I kept my eyes off Tolbukhin's glass, but I couldn't resist stealing a glance at Zheltov's when the WAC came around to fill it. Again a different carafe was sneaked from under an apron. As ill-luck would have it, Zheltov's beedy little eyes caught mine before I could bring them back to my plate.

"Marshal," Colonel General Zheltov said turning to Tolbukhin, "the American Lieutenant Colonel seems to have forgotten your advice."

"Four glasses fine," Tolbukhin roared.

When I'd choked them down, Alexander, who still didn't know what I'd been up to, said to his host, "Marshal, if you make the poor fellow drink any more fines, *I'm* going to be sick."

Although it had cost me seven glasses of vodka, I'd not only confirmed my suspicions, but had even obtained tacit confessions that our Russian hosts were quietly drinking water while they drowned their guests in vodka. Perhaps it's an old Soviet military custom. At all events it was information that proved very useful in the many inter-allied banquets that were to take place as the war drew to a close.

Conversation throughout breakfast was pretty desultory and I fear my translating, after all the vodka, didn't contribute to any meeting of minds. Field Marshal Alexander took the honors by proposing a toast in Russian which he'd learned during the Anglo-American expedition against the Soviets in Archangel during the Russian Revolution.

"Breakfast" over, the conference broke up into meetings of specialists.

While the specialists met, MacLean and I took a stroll through the village.

We'd gone about two hundred yards when a Soviet sentry wearing the red cap of the MVD appeared from nowhere and told us regretfully that it would not be possible to go any further.

"And why not?" we asked a little peevishly.

"There's no place to go," he answered simply.

"But we don't want to go anywhere. We just want to take a walk in the country."

"It's not good to walk in the country, and anyway there's no place to take a walk to."

We said we didn't want to walk *to* any place. We just wanted to walk around.

"Walk around? Then why don't you walk around inside the village? It's not so muddy. Look, there's a little garden with a path in the Main Square. You could walk around it."

"It's a little small, don't you think? We might get dizzy walking in such a small circle."

The guard decided we were making fun of him and began to get annoyed.

"I don't care where you walk or if you walk so long as you don't go past this point. Those are my orders and that's the way it's going to be until my boss tells me different!"

So we turned back in the opposite direction and got about four hundred yards when a second sentry stopped us with the same story. Then we retraced our steps and went up the main street past the Town Hall. Fifty feet beyond it a third sentry blocked the path.

The curious thing was that nowhere, as far as we could see, was there the slightest trace of Soviet military installations. Only one or two trucks stood in the barnyard behind Headquarters. Even the dusty streets showed no signs of heavy motor traffic.

Apparently Tolbukhin and a small staff had swept into the village a few hours before we arrived, complete with a mess unit and the prettiest WAC's he could find. They'd cleared the center of town of all local inhabitants (we never saw a single Hungarian in our brief stay), cleaned up the cottages, made up some beds and were ready to receive their distinguished foreign visitor. He'd gone Potemkin, Catherine the Great's Minister, one better. Potemkin had built fake villages along the road to please his mistress. Tolbukhin had taken a real village and made a fake Military Headquarters out of it. To please his distinguished Allies?

The meetings came to an end around four p.m. when Russians ordinarily have their big meal of the day. On this occasion it must have been the big meal of the month for we sat until eight in the evening, eating, toasting, drinking and speech-making.

Then Tolbukhin announced that there would be a special performance of Red Army entertainers at the Town Hall. For three more hours we listened to folk songs, watched folk dances and heard hymns of praise to Stalin.

Then Tolbukhin suggested a light snack before going to bed. We went back to his "Headquarters" cottage, drank more vodka and finally struggled off to bed. By this time the staff had suffered a few casualties. One British brigadier had slipped under the table during dinner. An aide was reported to have fallen through a window, though investigations later showed he'd merely toppled over on the window sill and knocked a flower pot into the village street. But those who had suffered most were the interpreters. By bedtime, my butter-eating proclivities left me the only one of the Russian-speakers more or less on his feet.

A Lieutenant General offered to take Alexander to his quarters and asked me to come along to interpret. The Field Marshal's quarters were in another peasant cottage, a hundred feet down the street, consisting of a bedroom and front room. As we walked in we found a charming blonde Russian WAC deep in sleep on a couch in the front room. Alexander looked at her and raised his eyebrows ever so slightly.

"Who, might I ask, is this?"

The Lieutenant General undertook to explain her away.

"I don't really know who she is or why she's here," he stammered. "Some sort of coincidence. As a matter of fact [he was thinking fast], she ordinarily lives in this cottage. Must have just come home by instinct."

Alexander's eyebrows came back to normal. "Like a homing pigeon?" he asked innocently.

"Exactly," said the Russian.

"In that case," Alexander continued, "do you suppose it would be possible to give her another little dove-cot for the night?"

The WAC was awakened and told she could find herself a bed elsewhere. Sleepily she got up from the couch and wandered off in the direction of the Town Hall.

When I got to my billet I found I was sharing General Lemnitzer's front room with another only slightly less charming WAC.

Lemnitzer was in the bedroom getting ready for bed.

"What the hell goes on here?" he asked. "What's the WAC for?"

I explained she was, ostensibly at least, there as an orderly. Lemnitzer looked unconvinced.

"Well, anyway, sir! She'll be sleeping in the outer room, so don't worry."

Still skeptical, Lemnitzer crawled into bed, and went to sleep.

In the front room the WAC had made up a bed for me on a couch and, like a children's nurse, tucked me in. I was charmed but very sleepy.

"Now just take this glass of hot milk and you'll be all right in the morning." She handed me a glass of milk, wrapped her overcoat about her and lay down on the floor at the foot of my bed.

Reveille was at five o'clock. A cold wet rag was mopping my forehead.

"Now up you get and you'll feel fine as soon as you've had breakfast. But first, I'll have to shave you."

As I dozed in a chair on the back porch, the WAC lathered and shaved me like a professional barber. Lemnitzer was already up and, a shade more cautious, had decided to shave himself.

"Now open your mouth," the WAC said, "and I'll brush your teeth."

But that was one step further than I cared to go.

Five minutes later, I accompanied Lemnitzer to the Headquarters cottage where we'd already had three feasts.

The rest of the staff were already present as I took my seat, the last of the guests.

"Late for breakfast, young man," Marshal Tolbukhin chuckled. "That'll be three cognacs—can't drink vodka before ten."

A WAC appeared with three wine glasses full of Soviet cognac. I gobbled two pads of butter, gulped the three glasses and waited to see what would happen. I hazily remember some herring, which I refused, and a large glass of champagne, which I think I swallowed. After that, all I'm sure of is that as "breakfast" ended, we went out and had our pictures taken. One of them (I have kept it as evidence) shows me still on my feet, a rather glazed expression in my eyes, a deathly grin hanging from my cheeks, leering over the shoulders of the Field Marshal and the Marshal.

The show in Tolbukhin's Potemkin Village Headquarters was over. The curtain went down. It didn't come up again, so far as I was concerned, till I got out of bed the next day in my own billet in Belgrade.

To this day there's one thing that puzzles me about that performance. Just what is there about a Soviet Military Headquarters that an ally can't be allowed to see? Is it so much more chaotic than an Allied Headquarters? Or have they some secret weapon that makes it less confusing? Or perhaps they don't have Army Group Headquarters—only a couple of truckloads of guards, dishes, food, vodka and pretty girls. In that case, Marshal Tolbukhin deserves another medal.

blondes and crippled bombers

one

of the jobs of our Mission was to round up the crews of American bombers who had crash landed or parachuted into Yugoslavia when their planes had been shot up on raids into Germany and her satellites. On the first day of our arrival in Valjevo a young American pilot had been brought in by the Partisans, sole survivor of a crew of ten, after parachuting from his crippled ship. Before we were done, more than a hundred airmen had been found and evacuated to Italy and thence home. Sometime when they managed to crash land without too much damage, we helped them get new engines from Italy, repair their planes and fly them back home. But that was more complicated and in all we only got six or eight Fortresses out that way, one of them lost with all hands on the way home from Belgrade.

Pilots flying missions that might bring them down over Yugoslavia had been carefully briefed about the friends and enemies they could expect to find in the welter of political ideologies below them. They were told that the Croatian terrorist Ustachi and the Croatian Nationalist Domobranci as well as Nazi Germans and Fascist Italians were bad medicine, but that Communist Partisans and Royalist Chetniks would help them to get out. With all the other things pilots had to learn in the course of their training, it was perhaps too much to expect that they would invariably remember all these nuances of Balkan politics as they tumbled earthward. We used to try to prepare maps indicating where the Chetniks were apt to be found and where the Partisans ruled the roost. But the situation changed so frequently that the maps were never very accurate. So there were a few mixups, and occasionally a crew would land in the middle of a Partisan area and demand to be taken to the Chetniks or vice versa.

Both Partisans and Chetniks prided themselves immensely on their records of evacuating Allied air crews, and when a crew got confused and asked to be taken to the rival camp, feelings were likely to be hurt. To add to the difficulty, some Partisans were convinced we were secretly helping Mikhailovich, the Chetnik leader, more than we were helping their man Tito. Whenever an air crew jumped to safety in Partisan territory and asked innocently for Mikhailovich, hell broke loose in Belgrade as soon as the news came through.

To make the situation still more complicated, the Partisans were constantly grousing because we still kept a Liaison Staff with the Chetniks. Arso, Tito's Chief of Staff, was particularly vehement on the subject. At the very first conference I had with him, he complained in the most truculent terms that the United States Liaison Officer with Mikhailovich, Colonel McDowell, was in fact organizing and taking part in Chetnik operations against the Partisans. To prove it, he offered to produce a pair of McDowell's pants captured by the Partisans in a recent engagement.

I hastened to point out that if McDowell had been directing the operation, he would certainly have found it more convenient to wear his pants. If the pants were actually his, it looked as though the Partisans had deliberately attacked the Chetniks, something they'd solemnly promised not to do. Arso, however, was unimpressed by my reasoning, and continued to demand McDowell's withdrawal on the ground that he was giving the Chetniks political prestige they didn't deserve.

Time after time, Tito, or his assistant, Bakic, or Olga would tell me:

"You dropped ten more men to Mikhailovich last night but we caught them."

Each time I'd remind them that ten men was the crew of a Fort and that, as had been demonstrated repeatedly, the ten-man secret mission was in all probability the crew of a damaged bomber. And each time they'd say:

"No, this case is different. They had papers telling them to go to the Chetniks. We're having them brought to Belgrade and this time we'll prove it."

And each time I'd explain the reason why airmen had instructions to go to either the Chetniks or Partisans.

And each time, after a lapse of two or three days, Olga or Bakic would call up and tell me sheepishly that the ten men had arrived in Belgrade and were, surprisingly enough, from a derelict bomber and were being sent up to our Mission for evacuation to Italy.

We fixed up a sort of dormitory for the crews to use while they waited for a plane to take them out. It was usually the gayest place in the Mission. There were always a few sprained or even broken ankles and sometimes more serious wounds lying about on the cots. But these didn't bother the

bandage wearers. They knew that they had survived the un-
certainties of a "mission," the explosion of the German flak
shell, the agonizing last glide of their doomed ship. Then the
order to jump and the fateful question: would it end in a
prison camp for the duration or would they land in the hands
of friendly guerrillas? And finally the long, hard trek over secret mountain trails to Belgrade. They'd survived it all, and
they knew that the next assignment for those who survived
was home leave in the U.S.A. While they waited they had
hot baths, soap, fresh uniforms, "Cokes," cigarettes and even
movies. Did they need anything more? All we had to do was
wire their boss, General Eaker, or his fabulous assistant in
charge of Air Crew Rescues, Colonel George Kraigher. *If*
there was anything the Airforce wouldn't do for its rescued
"boys," I never found out what it was.

Kraigher had been born in Slovenia and spoke Serbian
fluently. He had been a commercial pilot in America and by
the time the war started he had clocked about as many miles
of flying as anyone in the United States. For a while he had
flown President Roosevelt and other dignitaries. Then he'd
been shipped out to Italy and headed the rescue service for
stranded airmen. At the same time he flew innumerable risky
missions for OSS to Yugoslavia, Hungary, Rumania and
even to a secret landing strip in the heart of Hilter's empire
in Czechoslovakia. He had evacuated dozens of wounded Partisans and Chetniks to hospitals in Italy, and on one occasion
had practically saved Tito's life by flying him out of a tight
spot in Montenegro. If General Eaker was our Santa Claus,
old George Kraigher was all of his six reindeer put together.

One of our first requests was for a ten-ton truck. We
needed it, we explained, to carry airplane engines to stranded
bombers we were trying to salvage. Until then my friend,
Soviet General Kisiliev, had been lending me a Red Army
truck from time to time, but it was so often sick or busy

that salvage operations were sometimes delayed for weeks. Bombers were precious in those days and a week's loss was serious business. A slight hitch developed when the Airforce discovered you couldn't get a truck big enough to carry an engine into a plane. But Messrs. Eaker and staff had no shortage of imagination.

I soon got a message to say three planes would arrive the next morning. Two were carrying half of a ten-ton truck each that had been sawed in half. The third had a welding crew to glue it back together again. It was the biggest and best truck Belgrade had seen for years, and once or twice I even lent it to General Kisiliev for odd jobs around town. I figured it would help him keep the American Airforce in mind.

But the Partisans were having even greater troubles with transportation shortages than we. They had few if any trucks and no jeeps at all. Their big Russian brothers, for all their alleged virtues, weren't in a position to help, since practically all their own transport was American anyway. Time and again Tito and even Arso begged me to get them some jeeps. I wired AFHQ and Washington and Donovan and eventually a hundred jeeps and trailers were allotted to the Partisans. Tito was delighted. But how to get them to Belgrade? There was still a substantial force of Germans between us and the Dalmatian Coast. We sent a few around by sea to Saloniki and then up to Belgrade but they were half worn-out before they arrived.

"Ask Eaker if he won't bring the rest in by plane," Tito suggested. "He's a good egg and he might do it."

I sent on the request, but doubted that Eaker would provide planes to carry thirty jeeps and trailers all the way to Belgrade.

About that time Tito said he wanted to give some medals to the American air crews who had dropped supplies and evacuated wounded Partisans during the fighting in the woods.

Could we supply him the names of about seventy-five men who'd been particularly active in these operations? At the same time, Tito told me he wanted to give Eaker a medal for all his help.

I got a list of candidates from Italy, gave it to Tito and a few days later got the list of decorations back from him. When the decorations and citations reached Caserta, I got a blast from Bob Joyce, our political base man at Headquarters.

"Don't you know," he wired, "that you *always* add the General commanding the unit to the list of medal-getters? Where's your etiquette?"

I went to Colonel Bakic, Tito's Chief of Cabinet, and told him of my *faux pas*. In no time at all a very pretty medal was on its way to the General concerned.

Then Tito asked Eaker to come to Belgrade and receive his medal personally. A date was arranged, and at noon of the day of Eaker's arrival, the entire Supreme Command of the Partisan Army, under Arso Jovanovich, was at the airport together with a guard of honor to meet him. There was even an American flag, which I'd supplied myself, on the ruins of the control tower. Tito was about the only military dignitary not present. He wanted to greet the General on the Palace steps, he explained, and besides he'd lent me his only limousine to drive the General from the airport.

While we waited for Eaker's Flying Fortress to arrive, we chatted and stamped about the runway trying to keep our feet warm. Precisely at midday Arso looked at his watch and made a few rude remarks about being on time. I suggested he wasn't the soul of promptness himself, but he retorted that he didn't have all the technical equipment we Americans had.

"Why, I don't even have a jeep for myself!"

At that moment there was a hum of airplane engines in the air. We strained our eyes in the direction of the mountains to the west to try to pick up the silver Fortress. Instead, we saw a cloud of C-47's flying in perfect formation headed for the airport. A minute later they were rolling down the runway and lining up on the apron in front of us. The motors stopped, the doors opened and ramps were let down.

A young Airforce captain marched stiffly up to me, saluted and reported:

"Sir, thirty jeeps for Marshal Tito!"

I turned to Arso and translated.

Twenty minutes after the planes had appeared on the horizon the last one was hurtling down the runway for a take off. Alongside the control tower thirty jeeps were parked, all gassed up, in perfect alignment. (Contrary to standard AAF regulations, all the jeeps we carried by plane into guerrilla areas carried a full supply of gas in their tanks, just in case there was trouble on the landing strip and they had to make a quick getaway into the woods.)

I turned to Arso.

"That, General, is how it's done in the American Army."

Arso and his fellow generals couldn't contain themselves at the sight of the delectable jeeps.

They ran over to where they were parked, jumped into them and started driving madly all over the airfield, twisting, turning, racing, braking and shouting exuberantly at each other. They looked more like a bunch of kids in an amusement park than the General Staff of an Army.

A few moments later a big shiny silver Fortress appeared over the horizon and, after a lot of whistle-blowing and shouting, the jeeps were cleared off the runway and brought back to the control tower.

The Fortress landed and lumbered slowly up to the apron. The Guard of Honor came to attention. A staircase (homemade) was trundled up to the small door and Eaker and his staff stepped down. Introductions were made. The band played. The Guard was reviewed. Eventually Eaker climbed into Tito's limousine.

As we drove away, I turned to the General.

"That business with the jeeps was an inspiration. You couldn't have timed it better."

Eaker looked a little blank.

"Jeeps? What jeeps?"

"Those thirty jeeps your people just unloaded."

"Oh! The ones you asked me to fly over? When did they arrive?"

"Exactly half an hour ago while the entire General Staff was waiting for you."

"Well, isn't that a coincidence? I told my men to bring them over on the first clear day."

Either the General was a good actor, or he had an excellent public relations staff. I suspect it was a little of both.

One of Eaker's Public Relations staff was Tex McCrary, the man the Russians had detained or entertained when he tried to photograph the Danube bridges. After we'd got the General squared away, Tex came to my office looking a little distressed. "About the arrival at the airport . . ." he started.

"What was wrong? I thought everything went very well," I interrupted.

"But—the cameramen—there were no cameramen."

"What do you mean? There were a couple of Partisan photographers."

"No, not that. Still pictures are all right, but there were no movies. Where were your movie men?" Tex asked. "We always make movies of whatever our generals do."

"I'm afraid we haven't got that fancy yet."

"You mean you don't even have a camera unit?" Tex asked in amazement.

"Certainly not. Where the hell would we get one from?"

Tex looked flabbergasted. "I thought every outfit had a camera unit."

I explained we were a very proletarian outfit.

"Well, as soon as we get back to Italy," Tex said, "I'll see what I can do."

He did and a few days later I got a wire from him saying a combat camera team complete with movie cameras, still cameras, klieg lights, generators, jeeps, trailers and even its own C-47 had been assigned to us for the duration. Tex made a special trip over to introduce them.

It sounds good, having your own combat camera team, but it does have its drawbacks. For one thing it was so much grander than the Mission that it rapidly developed the characteristics of a tail wagging a dog.

Every morning thereafter the captain of the team would report to my office. "Anything to be filmed today, sir?"

We filmed Tito in black and white and color. We filmed him at his desk, in his library, riding a horse, playing with his dog, Tiger. He was very patient and I have a sneaking suspicion he rather enjoyed it.

We filmed Partisan infantry, sitting, marching, fighting. We filmed Partisan artillery and cavalry trotting and galloping.

I was running dry of ideas to keep the camera team busy when Tex came to the rescue.

"Planning to do a documentary on the Partisan guerrilla war," he wired me. "As soon as we have the scenario complete will let you know what sequences we'll need from you."

It was just about the time "Fighting Lady" had been released and I think every Public Relations Officer in the Army was dreaming of another hit film with his own outfit in the leading role.

I cabled Tex we'd be delighted. "Just tell us what you

want," I wired, "and we'll shoot all the footage you need."

Now that we were going into the movie business, it gave me a certain feeling of importance to talk about "shooting" and "footage." The camera team captain gave me a few more technical expressions which I threw around indiscriminately.

But producing motion pictures I soon discovered isn't as easy as you might think.

First Tex wanted a lot of pretty Partisan girls dancing the "Kola," a native folk dance, around a bonfire. As all the Partisan girls were busy fighting, we rounded up a lot of Belgrade's golden youth after they'd hauled their daily quota of rubble, took them out to what had been the Belgrade Golf Club and the camera captain "shot" to his heart's content. We didn't tell the dancers they were supposed to represent Partisans or they might not have played. (They still thought the Partisans were a passing fad and would soon be replaced by someone who would appreciate their social position.) "Just be peasants," we told them. They found that a little beneath their dignity, but we gave them some free smokes and drinks and they eventually agreed.

Then Tex wired for a "sequence" of a pretty Partisan blonde crawling through thick underbrush with a rifle.

You'd be surprised how hard it is to get any girl to be filmed crawling through thick underbrush with a rifle. For a pretty Royalist Belgrade blonde, it ranks with worse than death. We finally persuaded our pretty blonde by telling her she was playing the role of a Chetnik spy infiltrating a Partisan camp, in disguise. That did the trick and we sent Tex yards of "footage" of her in the underbrush around Belgrade's abandoned golf club.

I never found out what happened to the film. Spring was well underway, the war was rapidly drawing to an end and I suspect the fancies of the young colonels on Eaker's staff were turning to thoughts of other things than guerrilla wars. Any-

way, it wasn't long before Tex went home and got married to
Jinx Falkenberg. Our poor deluded Royalist blonde from Belgrade had apparently crawled through the underbrush for
nothing.

The evening of Eaker's arrival, Tito gave him a large banquet and the medal. There were innumerable speeches and
toasts as usual and after the banquet there was a movie and
some folk dancing. After that all the guests danced with Olga
and the two or three other ladies of Tito's entourage.

It was very late when we got home but not too late for Tex
McCrary to go out on a reconnaissance mission to get some
first hand intelligence on the night life in Belgrade. He was
sharing my apartment but I was asleep long before he came
back.

The next morning I was in my office discussing the final
details of the lunch we were to give that day for Eaker and
Tito, with Mike Yovanovich our man of all— or almost all—
trades. Mike turned himself inside out for Field Marshal Alexander but for Santa Claus Eaker he was really performing
miracles. For days the yard had been a mooing, grunting,
cackling mass of calves, pigs, sheep, geese and ducks. Now
they were all slaughtered and in the hands of Stepan, the chef.

Suddenly Tex McCrary burst into my office in his under-
pants. A pair of slightly bloodshot eyes were popping out
from behind a half-lathered face.

"Good God, man, there's a fish in the bathtub! It's enormous." Tex stretched out his arms full length. "As long as
that."

Mike sidled out of the room in the direction of the bathroom.

I smiled sympathetically and said, "Nonsense, there's no
fish in the bathtub."

"Damn it, I tell you there *is* a fish in the bathtub. Come

and look at it. I tell you it's a real fish. See for yourself." He practically dragged me from my chair.

As we reached the bathroom door he burst in ahead of me, pointed to the tub and said "Look." I looked and so did he.

The bathtub was empty.

I offered Tex some sedative or a bromoseltzer. I even suggested sending for the Mission doctor to examine him. But Tex stuck to his guns. Eventually he calmed down enough to eat a little breakfast and go about his duties with General Eaker, but he wasn't his usual bustling self.

I had a lot of work to do that morning and was glad to get rid of him with his shouts of "Fish!" First I had to finish with Mike and the menu. Mike was a very good feeder and, besides knowing something about good food, he liked to see lots of it on the table. So I spent a half hour vainly trying to get him to cut out one of the eight courses.

Then there was the head of Tito's personal bodyguard who came to call about the security arrangements during the lunch. He said they had already cordoned off a "small area" of several blocks around the Mission and had plain-clothes men and sentries on all the street corners, but they would like to put a few guards inside the house, in the cellar and on the roof if I didn't object.

Tito still had plenty of enemies in Belgrade and the so-called Chetnik underground had been threatening to assassinate him and take to the woods in revolt "as soon as the leaves got green." The Green Leaf was their symbol. (They'd recently sent one to a member of the Mission, Mike Petrovich, much to his distress. He didn't know whether it meant they were soliciting his sympathy or putting the finger on him.) So I told the bodyguard he could put all the guards around he wanted, provided he'd relieve me of any responsibility for Tito's health. He could send a doctor into the kitchen, too, if he wanted. I remembered Molotov always had done that in Moscow when he went out for dinner. But Tito never went that far.

Then we had to arrange our own Honor Guard at the entrance. We didn't have any smart M.P.'s with snow-white helmets and silk kerchiefs and pipe-clayed gaiters. We didn't have any regular rifles. We didn't even have any soldiers who knew the manual of arms. But we managed to borrow a couple of pairs of white cotton gloves from one of the waiters at the Majestic Hotel and we got a couple of special service OSS carbines slicked up.

The Mission's executive officer, a very military, eager Marine, Captain Bill Cary, took two of the radio operators into the back yard, put them through a fast course in how to present arms, and posted them at the front entrance. After that I asked him to go and see if he couldn't arrange to put some flowers in the reception room and get the fire lighted in the open fireplace.

Just before our guests arrived, I made a last minute check-up to see that all was in order. When I got to the reception room I found a bunch of posies wilting in front of a roaring fire and turned impatiently on Captain Cary.

"Damn it, Bill, I asked for some fresh flowers and you stick some weeds there that look as though they were from last year's basement sale."

The unfortunate Marine Captain drew himself to attention and stared straight at me till I'd finished my outburst. Then in a low voice, trembling with indignation, he answered:

"Colonel, may I just say, sir, [he underlined the "sir"] that I didn't join the Marines to be anybody's God-damn flower girl!"

It was the finest exhibition of righteous Marine wrath I'd ever seen. Meekly, I threw the wilted flowers into the fire and told Bill to forget it.

The Marshal arrived a bit early, and there was a certain

amount of struggling with undersized gloves by the Honor
Guard but they turned out a most presentable salute, thanks
to Bill Cary's training, and if all the gloves weren't exactly
buttoned, Tito was kind enough not to notice it.

The luncheon went off well, as such occasions always did
under Mike's supervision. We had a few slivovitz's in the
flowerless reception room before going in to eat. I thought I
saw Tex knock his slivovitz's back with a good deal of relish.
He still looked a bit shaky and I tried to keep the conversation
steered away from the subject of fish.

After the caviar and soup courses, Mike Yovanovich
marched in with a tremendous sturgeon on a platter so big
that it took all Mike's strength to manage it. I stole a glance
at Tex. He seemed to go a shade whiter. Then slowly some
color crept into his cheeks.

"Charlie," he called across the table, "don't I recognize
that fish?"

"Perhaps," I said, "but if you Airforce people won't give
us iceboxes where can you store fish except in the bathtub?"

General Eaker not only provided us with airplane rides,
extra cigarettes, jeeps, trucks and combat camera teams. He
also gave us Thornton Wilder.

We were hardly established in Belgrade before the battle
for Belgrade's minds started. Tito began it by immediately
banning, as was to be expected, the old quisling newspaper
Novo Vremene (New Times) and putting in its place a Communist Party paper called *Borba* (Battle) which looked and
read so exactly like *Pravda*, Moscow's Communist paper, that
you could scarcely tell the difference. The only trouble was
that Belgrade's rather stubborn reading public didn't take to
it very well. To try to stimulate sales, the newsboys on the
street started shouting:

"Read *Borba*, the new version of *Novo Vremene*."

The newsboys were soon asked to "volunteer" for a quick refresher course in dialectic materialism.

The Russians got into the game by opening a reading room full of busts of Stalin and Lenin and *Pravdas* and *Izvestijas*. They even gave the starved movie theaters of Belgrade some Soviet films. But the Russians developed the disconcerting habit of asking from time to time for their films back to show to their troops, just as a theater owner had sold out his house for a showing.

Thereupon OWI decided it would be a good idea to have some free showings of first class American films in Belgrade. For their first attempt they sent over "Song of Bernadette," not precisely the best choice for a city in the throes of a political struggle in which the religious issue played a prominent part. So we asked the head of OWI in Bari, Reid, to join us on the spot to see if he couldn't do better.

Reid, with Mike Yovanovich's help, promptly got hold of one of the best show windows on Belgrade's main street and began to fix up an American reading room. When it was all ready, we passed out invitations to every Partisan Bigwig in town to a grand opening exhibition of our Information Center. Everyone but Tito turned up for the event, plus a rather large contingent of uninvited guests from the Secret Police. The appearance of the latter puzzled us a little, until some friendly soul pointed out that our invitation to the opening exhibition of the American Information Center had been translated to read "An exhibition of an American Intelligence Agency." So I made a short speech in atrocious Serb apologizing for the error. Most of our guests were understanding enough, but the Secret Police were clearly disgruntled and soon left the party.

The Russian counter-move was to bring troupes of ballerinas, sopranos, and folk dancers from Moscow. I helped them choose their performers, but my best friends from Moscow days were not necessarily Moscow's best dancers. Nevertheless, they tried hard and pleased the few Partisan élite who were allowed to see them.

Reid's next move was to get some films slightly more suited to the times than "Song of Bernadette" and distribute them to the theaters throughout town with the promise that, unlike the Russians, we wouldn't ask for them back in the middle of a performance. Although the films were not always the most intellectually stimulating works of art, they kept the majority of Belgraders amused and aware that Hollywood was still out in front.

But our real triumph on the battle front for minds was Thornton Wilder. He'd been on General Eaker's staff for some time and we had asked if he couldn't be detailed to us. Wilder was enthusiastic and General Eaker, as usual, readily agreed.

We gave a big reception to Belgrade's intellectual set, who for years had been completely cut off from the West, and triumphantly produced Wilder whose writings were well known in Yugoslavia. I can't say that Wilder made any great dent on the out-and-out Communists in town, but among the remaining ninety-five percent he was received with open arms. He was invited to speak at reading clubs; literary teas were arranged; and day after day Wilder went around tirelessly telling Belgrade what had been happening in French, British and American literature since the war broke out.

When the Russians tried to meet the challenge with some popular Soviet "realist writers" like Fadeyev and Simenov with their hymns to Stalin, it was really hardly a contest. The Fadeyevs and Simenovs drew their appropriate applause from appropriate circles but as one well known Yugoslav writer told us, "Wilder's the first fresh air we've had since Hitler came."

in the middle of March, the British Ambassador to Yugoslavia, Stevenson, arrived. A week later the Soviet Ambassador, Sadchikov, turned up. In the absence of an Ambassador of our own, I asked for an appointment to call first on Stevenson and then on Sadchikov.

Stevenson promptly asked me around for a drink. Sadchikov didn't answer. On the assumption that his secretary either hadn't got my message or couldn't read, I went around to the Soviet Embassy to find a belligerent young soldier with a rifle blocking my way. I'd had lots of them to deal with by then and I told him, first, to salute me and, second, if he wouldn't let me pass, to fetch someone with a rank sufficiently high for me to talk to. The sentry saluted and disappeared into the building. A moment later a distraught secretary came out full of apologies and rushed me into the Embassy. Inside, he led me to a pair of imposing double doors and, without knocking, hustled me into a dark room where, once my eyes got used to the lack of light, I saw my friend, General Kisiliev, Ambassador Sadchikov and a third individual huddled over a coffee table spread with documents.

My unannounced entry had the effect of a quarterback's signal to jump from the huddle to the playing positions. The documents on the coffee table vanished. Sadchikov leaped behind a desk. Kisiliev spurted to his playing position in an easy chair, and the third man slunk into a dark corner like the key man in a shoestring play.

I apologized for my abrupt entry but explained I was expecting to be shown into a waiting room, not a secret den. Kisiliev giggled. Sadchikov smiled. A hollow laugh came from the man hidden in the dark corner.

In a moment Sadchikov had recovered himself and ushered me over to a couch as far from his desk as possible. Almost immediately a bottle of vodka and a bowl of caviar appeared on the coffee table, as mysteriously as the documents had vanished from it. We exchanged a few polite remarks. The man in the corner gradually regained his courage. Like a shy, wild animal, he stealthily made his way to the table and sat down, still keeping well in the shadows. A moment later he summoned up his courage and took a glass of vodka.

The conversation revolved closely around the weather in Belgrade and other non-revolutionary themes. The man in the dark, fortified by the vodka, spoke in English.

"And where did you learn your excellent English?" I asked.

"You taught me," came the voice from the shadow. "In Washington in 1936. I'm Dimitri Antonovich Chuvakhin," he added.

Straining my eyes through the gloom I recognized a former

attaché of the Soviet Embassy in Washington who had come to me once, explaining he knew no language but Russian and couldn't find anyone to talk to. In those days it was still relatively safe for a Soviet diplomat to call on a foreigner in Washington without being shot for deviationism. I had invited him to my apartment several times and had even found him an English teacher.

In spite of the caviar and vodka, the conversation soon began to die on the vine. It was obvious Sadchikov's Embassy wasn't going to differ much from the other morbid tombs that represented Soviet Russia abroad. After a few inconsequential exchanges of repartee, I left. Needless to say, the call was never returned by anyone, including my ex-pupil, and I never went to the Soviet Embassy again.

Following the Russian and British example, Washington decided it was time for the Military Mission to make way for an Embassy. Eventually the State Department ordered an Ambassador to report to Belgrade.

But before he arrived, there was still a job or two to be done.

Appropriately enough, Zemun Airfield, my first headache, became one of my last as well. The American Air Transport Command was very anxious to set up some facilities there so that they could use it as a stop on routes they hoped to establish to the East, where the war was still going strong. The British wanted facilities for the same purpose.

The Russians, on the contrary, didn't ask for any facilities for two rather simple reasons. In the first place Russian airlines don't need "facilities," like weather stations, groundcontrol landing facilities, navigation beacons, and so forth. In such matters Soviet civil aviation is still in the Brushwood Boy stage. In the second place, the Russians figured that they didn't need to ask Tito for privileges at Zemun. They had liberated the field for him and if they needed anything particular at any time they wouldn't bother to ask for it.

One bright day the head of ATC for Europe, General Hoag, blew into Zemun without a clearance, but with a half dozen chicken colonels, to explain how many G.I.'s he needed to maintain the minimum facilities. As a matter of routine, I'd sent word to the field when the General arrived that without clearance he wasn't legally allowed to land. But within a half hour he and his colonels were seated around my desk, telling me in no uncertain terms why they needed Tito's permission to have seventy men in Belgrade.

I explained there was a very slight possibility that Tito might let a small contingent operate a weather and signal service, but that anything like seventy men smacked too much of an invasion.

But seventy, they said, was the smallest unit they ever operated with.

"What do they all do?" I asked.

"Well, there are fifteen weather men, including seven experts, and eight clerks," they began.

"Why can't you use Yugoslavs as clerks?"

ATC's weather colonel looked surprised.

"But we never use natives," he explained. "Besides they wouldn't know English."

"I'm afraid it's not a question of what you've ever done before. It's a question of whether you can get along with a few men or not come at all. Plenty of Yugoslavs speak English."

It was the same with the signal staff—five operators and six helpers. I suggested they recruit the helpers locally.

But the worst was the "administrative staff."

"We'll need a chief for the unit with secretary, a deputy with secretary, and executive with secretary and then the actual services staff: a service officer to supervise the billets, the mess, the guard, the motor pool, and the P.X. Then we'll need an officer for each of those jobs individually plus a mess sergeant, a cook, two assistant cooks; a security unit of twenty-four M.P.'s and a medical unit of four."

I tried to imagine how Tito would react to this proposal, and gulped.

"As I understand it, you need twelve expert weather and radio experts plus fourteen non-technical assistants to do the actual work. To keep them fed, et cetera, you'll need forty-four more men."

"But they've got to eat," said the mess colonel.

"Couldn't they use a Yugoslav cook?" I asked.

"But they can't eat native grub," the mess colonel protested.

"I suggest you have dinner with me tonight and then explain why not," I retorted.

"But G.I.'s aren't used to native grub," he argued.

"The men in our mission have gotten used to it pretty quickly. Ask any of them whether they'd rather eat here or in the Army mess in Bari."

The argument continued hot and heavy for several hours. When the smoke cleared away, we had settled on a temporary contingent of seventeen men, to be reduced to twelve in a month's time as soon as Yugoslav assistants could be trained. I promised to try to sell this to Tito first thing in the morning.

Next day I went to see Tito at the White Palace. Since the formation of the Government, Tito was growing less and less accessible and I was told I could take my business to his Chief of Cabinet, Colonel Bakic. I knew Bakic couldn't give me a decision, but reluctantly I went to his office. There I found Tito with him. Tito said "Hello" very civilly, and made for the door. I did an end run and got there just ahead of him. With my back to the door, I told him as briefly as I could what we wanted. Tito hesitated. There were too many foreigners at Zemun already, he said. The British wanted twenty men. We wanted seventeen more.

Hastily I repeated all the ATC arguments that I'd been refuting the evening before. Tito looked at his watch. He wanted to get out but he wasn't going to be impolite. I told him the Americans were already carrying ninety percent of his traffic with the west. If he refused, his officials and mail and couriers might suddenly find it impossible to get out. Now that the fighting was almost over (it was April 1945), ATC simply wasn't going to run any more shoestring lines. Tito got the point.

"O.K., seventeen men for a month and twelve thereafter. Arrange the details with Bakic. Now may I go? I've a most important engagement."

I thanked him and took my hand off the door knob.

It was also time to close out my accounts in Belgrade, financial and otherwise.

Twelve years with the State Department had impressed me with the enormous importance of accounts, though it never taught me how to render them. The State Department, the Accountant General's Office, the Treasury and the Congress don't see eye to eye with me on the matter, but I've tried to humor them. They operate on the philosophy that, though they can send you to the ends of the earth and rely on your judgment in making up policies, safeguarding their interests, and disposing of millions of dollars in loans, and so on, yet they can't trust you for the price of a Pullman ticket unless you turn in the stub.

In Belgrade I was bombarded by the Accountant General's Office with thoroughly incomprehensible forms in which the sum of $41 kept reappearing with vague indications that it had something to do with my accounts for the Legation in

Kabul, Afghanistan, three years before. There was a lot of rhetoric about debits and credits, but whether they owed me or I owed them was not stated. I filed the forms away in the scrap basket. After all, they'd waited three years, they could probably wait till the shooting stopped.

After the war I asked an expert in Government accounting to decipher them for me. He reported that I'd apparently overpaid a clerk who had been sent to Kabul from Japan in 1942 by $41. So I sent $41 to the Treasury.

But the same forms kept right on coming, angrily demanding that I do something. As usual, they weren't very clear about what they wanted me to do. I decided I'd give them the silent treatment again and let them cool off for a while.

Two years more elapsed. Each month the same forms reached me. I just waited.

Then in 1950 a letter came from the Treasury enclosing a check for $41. It had all been a mistake, they said.

In the OSS things were different. When you set out on a mission, the last thing they used to do to you before strapping on your parachute was give you a money belt loaded with Louis d'Or gold pieces.

"If you need more, just radio us," they'd say expansively.

After you've carried a couple of dozen Louis d'Ors in a money belt for a month, the last thing you want to do is ask for more. Out in the woods with the Partisans I found them almost useless but some of our sub-missions, which I was apparently supposed to finance, scattered over hundreds of miles of Balkan mountains, every now and then had an opportunity to do some shopping. Occasionally a courier would come panting up to the Mission with a letter from a sub-mission chief saying he was fresh out of Louis', could he have a couple? The letter generally enclosed a chit of paper reading "IOU 2 Louis, (signed) C 318." I'd gladly lighten my stomach muscles of two Louis' and pocket the chit.

Nevertheless, it seemed to me, with my State Department indoctrination, that this was a dangerous business. Suppose, as happened from time to time, C 318 or his courier got caught by the Germans. I could just see the pile of forms that would glut my mail for decades while I tried to explain the chit. So one evening I composed a radio message to Headquarters suggesting that they figure out a system to pay the sub-missions so the chits could be redeemed. I told them the matter wasn't urgent, but that they might want to give it some thought with a view to a possible Congressional investigation when the war was over. But Headquarters wasn't going to let grass grow under its feet. By return radio contact came an urgent message.

"Dropping $5,000 in gold to you tonight." And they did.

It didn't solve my problem in the slightest and it made my money belt so heavy that I was practically immobilized for the duration, but it was irrefutable proof I wasn't working for the State Department any more.

Fortunately we soon got to Belgrade and I was able to put my money belt in a field safe.

Then came the problem of financing the Mission. Until then everything we'd needed had naturally been supplied by Tito's commissary. Now, however, the Partisans figured we could start supporting ourselves.

This change was, of course, part and parcel of the shift in the Partisan Party line as the Russians got closer and the need for help from the West seemed to diminish in the eyes of some of the less astute of Tito's colleagues. One of our first inklings of the change involved a dozen cots.

In the woods, before Tito turned up, I'd got into the habit of going to Arso, the Chief of Staff, with our problems. Arso had been a professional soldier before the war and apparently had been as uninterested in politics as a Balkan army officer can be. But after resistance to Hitler collapsed, he took to the woods, joined Tito and over night became more Marxian than Marx. He was a sour sullen sort of fellow, the exact opposite of the affable Tito. He took his rank and position very seriously and made no secret of the contempt he felt for allied Military Mission Chiefs with the mere rank of Lieutenant Colonel. By the time we got to Belgrade he made himself practically inaccessible and let it be known that anything the Americans had to ask could be put in writing. So I went to Tito and put my problem to him.

Unfortunately by that time my list of problems, many of them trivial, was a long one. Tito began to get impatient.

"Colonel," he said when he thought my list of troubles was exhausted, "is there any chance that one day you'll come in with an item or two of good news?"

I replied that I hoped so, but that much depended on himself. Besides, I still had one matter that was causing serious trouble in my own Mission.

"Well, what is it?" Tito said, a little bored and fed up.

"It's a question of beds," I told him. "We need twelve beds very badly."

"Beds!" roared Tito indignantly. "What do you mean by coming to the Marshal of Yugoslavia with a complaint like that? Go see the Liaison Staff or go to Arso! The idea of bothering me because a dozen American soldiers haven't got beds!"

"No, Marshal," I replied, "that isn't the point. I've asked the Liaison Staff ten times and Arso five. Arso won't even answer me. Anyway, the beds aren't for the Americans. We're all quite used to sleeping on the floor. But those Partisan soldiers you insist on assigning to me as 'guards' seem to have changed a bit since they've come out of the woods. At least they claim they'll catch rheumatism if they have to sleep on the floor any longer. You see my difficulty? I should hate to have Arso accuse me of causing the desertion of a squad of his soldiers. But what can I do?"

Tito smiled. He reached for the phone and got his Chief of Staff on the wire. "Arso, what's all this about no beds for the American Mission? Do you mean to say after all the Americans have done for us you can't find a dozen cots for them? Don't you know how to behave in polite company? Get them those beds at once."

He slammed the receiver dramatically.

"That'll take care of Arso," he said, "and if you ever have any more problems you come straight to me. Don't bother with the General Staff any more. They don't seem to understand even the elementary principles of politics."

Needless to say I never got the beds from Arso, but I never had any more difficulty bringing my problems to Tito or to his personal assistant, Colonel Bakic. The incident was also revealing as it related to Arso and his concept of "elementary principles of politics." When the war was over, Arso was sent to the Red Army Staff College in Moscow and when he returned he was made Chief of the new Yugoslav Military Academy. Apparently he considered the appointment beneath his prestige and sulked in his tent for several years. When Tito began to have difficulties with Stalin, Arso put his money on Moscow. But something went wrong with his calculations and he had to take to his heels with two other anti-Tito conspirators. Their plan was to pretend they were going hunting along the Rumanian border, skip across the frontier and thence to Moscow. But again something went wrong. As they approached the frontier they were challenged by a Partisan frontier guard. Instead of answering the challenge and "pulling rank" on the unfortunate guard, Arso lost his head and started to shoot. The guard shot back—rather better than Arso did. Arso was killed instantly.

In spite of Arso, the Partisans continued to supply us with

food for a time but eventually, as food became harder to ex-
tract from the peasants, our rations got thinner and thinner.
We could buy what food we needed from the peasants, but
marketing with Louis d'Or proved a little impractical. You
couldn't just chip off a dram of gold every time you bought
some fresh lettuce. You could sell the gold on the black market for dinars but there's no better way of getting into trouble than that—or at least so the State Department used to say.

Being no financier myself I turned the problem over to
Fred Yeiser, our Indianapolis Music Critic, whose specialty
was Order of Battle. His Partisan opposite member was Major General Klisanic with whom he spent hours each day
piecing together the little hints and clues about where this or
that division was and what shape it was in. Klisanic was a
very smart fellow but had not previously had much experience
in Battle Order work so he welcomed Fred's assistance and
tactful instruction. One day Yeiser explained to Klisanic the
rank insignia of various armies, including the United States
Army. When he was through, Klisanic seemed a little puzzled and staring at his instructor's sleeve said, "But that would
make you only a sergeant." Fred blushed prettily and complimented the General on his quickness at learning.

But little by little Battle Order intelligence began to peter
out—doubtless at Arso's instructions. He probably thought in
his usual tortuous way that what the Americans didn't know
wouldn't hurt them. Perhaps, too, he figured we might discover there weren't quite as many German divisions on the
southeastern front as Stalin had claimed at Yalta. Only once
had he volunteered any information to me about the enemy
troops on his own front.

He had just begun to discover that in the matter of supplies
the Russians weren't quite the Santa Clauses he'd expected.
So he called me and asked whether Eaker wouldn't give him
some equipment he desperately needed. I wasn't very recep-

tive and to butter me up he had taken me to his operations room and shown me the current line-up on the front. He pointed to two enemy cavalry divisions prominently marked on the map.

"They're the Cossack Divisions," he explained. "They were recruited by the Germans from Russian Prisoners of War and they're the toughest two outfits we've been up against since the front was stabilized. On their horses they are more mobile than any mechanized divisions in the mountains and they fight like hell."

"That reminds me, General," I interrupted. "I've had instructions from Washington to ask you to let me know at once if you ever come across even a single squad of Americans fighting on the side of the enemy."

Arso's eyes blazed and his thin hard jaws snapped as he reached up and pulled the curtain down over his top secret map. It was the last time I ever saw it. Nor did he see the special equipment he so badly wanted from us.

With no more Order of Battle to puzzle over, time was beginning to hang heavy on Yeiser's hands when I made him our Mission Financier. Fred said he didn't know anything about finances but he was willing to learn. So he went down to the National Bank, which Tito had just taken over, and had a talk with the new Director. He explained that he had a certain amount of gold. The Director's ears pricked up: that was one thing he didn't have and though he didn't know much about finances either, he did know that every respectable National Bank had a gold reserve. So Fred and the bank did a dicker and Fred loaned them the coveted "gold reserve" in exchange for some dinars. Everyone was happy and Fred came home with a large stock of dinars and an IOU for the gold, all as legal as you could ask. The dinars lasted us a month or more. When the till was running low, I asked Fred what to do. Did we need any more gold?

"Hell, no," said Fred, "we still own the entire national gold reserve of Yugoslavia, and the dinar rate has dropped 100 points. I've a vague idea we can make something of it."

So Fred went back to his friend the Director, dickered a bit, and came back with some more dinars.

"But what about the gold?"

"Oh, I loaned it back to the bank."

It was all way over my head, but seemed eminently satisfactory to all concerned, especially the National Bank.

Now that I was about to leave I dutifully sent in my accounts to the Finance Officer and asked for an audit.

A day or so later I got a wire:

"Your accounts show that after deducting expenditures, the Mission has $2,000 more dollars than it started with. Explain."

I called in Yeiser. "Explain," I said.

Yeiser looked at the cable and wrinkled his forehead. Finally he burst out:

"Hell, Colonel, I can't *explain* it. I'm just a music critic."

I told the Finance Office as much and suggested they stop asking silly questions.

Eventually the Ambassador and his staff arrived. As best we could, we "briefed" him on the rather complex political situation in Belgrade. Then I took him in my jeep up to the White Palace and introduced him to Tito. Finally we arranged a series of dinners and receptions to introduce him to the Cabinet and Foreign Ministry officials, the Army and the Press.

Just before I left, the Ambassador said he wanted to see some fighting. So, reluctantly, because I don't like seeing fighting, I drove him in a jeep to the Srem front where the Partisans were gradually pressing the Germans back to the northwest.

We reached a good-sized town in the Srem about lunch time. Peko Dapcevic of the First Corps met us and explained that they'd only just captured the place after a hard night's fight.

"It wasn't the Germans who caused the most trouble but the local Ustachi [Quisling] militia who knew their number was up if we captured the place," Peko explained. "They took off their uniforms and every time we got close they just pretended they were peasants. But when we turned our backs they grabbed their rifles and shot the devil out of us. It's a dirty business. But we caught a dozen of them with rifles in their hands and we'll make an example of them."

Peko fed us a good lunch and took us for a tour of the front. We got up to within a couple of hundred yards of the German lines, but then they must have caught sight of us for several mortar shells lobbed over and landed beside the narrow path that had been cleared through the mine field. We ducked into a trench and when the mortar fire quieted down, we slipped back to town where Peko gave us a glass of slivovitz to speed us on our way.

Just before we started off, Peko had an idea. "Would you like to see those Ustachi we caught? They're right nearby."

The Ambassador said he would.

We were ushered into a stone cottage, heavily guarded by Partisans. In a big bare room stood a dozen husky peasants in civilian clothes. As we came in a Partisan sentry called "Attention" and they slowly stood up, leaning heavily against the four walls. Peko talked to one or two of them, while I translated for the Ambassador. They were local farmers, they told us, and had been enlisted in the Croat Ustachi by Ante Pavlic's men from Zagreb.

Had they fought the Partisans? Yes.

Had they worn uniforms? Up till yesterday they had but when things got hot they took them off.

Then they'd fought in civilian clothes? Yes.

Did they know the penalty for that? Yes.

A great big giant among them began to wobble. His knees buckled and he slid to the floor. The corporal of the guard shook him and told him to stand up.

Feeling slightly ill, I made for the door.

One of the Americans in the party, who had come to Yugoslavia with the Ambassador, asked Peko what they were going to do with the prisoners. Peko pointed his finger at his head and cocked his thumb.

The American turned to me in surprise.

"Are they going to *shoot* them? They mustn't do that! Why, they're just a different political party, like the Republicans."

I'm afraid my explanation of the difference between politics on Capitol Hill and in the Balkans was a little curt.

Driving home we'd reached the main highway from Novi Sad to Belgrade, when we passed three small civilian cars, evidently all of them broken down. Around them hovered a half dozen Orthodox priests. They were of rather high rank, judging by their elaborate robes, the enormous bucket-like hats perched on their heads and the yards of black drapes that flowed behind them.

I was driving the jeep with the Ambassador beside me. At a signal from one of the priests I pulled up.

"Excuse me," he said in Russian. "I am the Patriarch of all the Russias."

He rolled off the title as though he were saying, "My name's Smith."

I translated for the Ambassador who understandably looked a little startled.

"Really? Tell him I'm the Ambassador of all the United States."

The Patriarch bowed low and stretched out his hand with great dignity.

"It is an honor," he said simply.

He went on to explain that he was on a visit to Yugoslavia from Moscow and that his party had been driving from Novi Sad to Belgrade when the cars they were in all broke down at once. He had an urgent appointment in Belgrade with the Metropolitan Josef. We seemed to have some room on the two little tin boxes on either side of the back seat—could we possibly let him and his secretary, Bishop Alexei, sit on them as far as Belgrade?

The Ambassador had no objection. But I took one look at those long silky black beards and the longer silkier black scarfs, and I remembered how Isadora Duncan had been strangled to death by getting her veil caught in the wheel of her car.

I got out two large G.I. army blankets and asked the Patriarch and his secretary, the Bishop, to get well wrapped up in them, beards, skirts, veils and all. I didn't tell them about Isadora Duncan. I was afraid they might not understand. I merely said it might be chilly.

Submissively they wrapped themselves up, till all you could see were their large black bucket hats and their wild dark eyes peering from the folds of the army blankets. They clambered over the sides of the jeep and off we went over the bumpy road to Belgrade.

It seemed to me singularly appropriate that my last job in Yugoslavia should be to bring the head of Russia's Orthodox Church to Belgrade, in a jeep, wrapped in a huge U. S. Army blanket.

nuts! he's no VIP ELEVEN

when

I arrived in Caserta after leaving Belgrade for the last time, I found a splendid battle raging at AFHQ between the political generals and political advisors on one hand and the generals' generals and the generals' political advisors on the other.

The question was whether to take two divisions away from General Clark's forces, then about to win the Battle of the Po, and send them to Trieste as fast as they could push the Germans back up the Adriatic coast. The generals' generals insisted that it would be a pity to slow up the Po victory by diverting divisions to the east on a purely political wild goose chase. The political generals argued that when the smoke cleared away, Trieste would turn out to be much more important than the Po. For if the Partisans got to Trieste first, it would take a lot of doing even to get them out again.

Field Marshal Alexander listened quietly to the roars on both sides, and eventually the Adriatic flank was reenforced with a Division or two. It wasn't enough to prevent all the trouble we later had in Trieste with the Partisans, but in the end it was enough to get some sort of solution. It was also enough to make the generals' generals who maintained that the only object of war was to win battles, grind their molars with rage. The only people who expressed no views were the unfortunate Triestinos. The hundred days they stayed under Yugoslav occupation is not the brightest chapter in the History of World War II.

After contributing what little I could to the confusion, I went on to Washington to be briefed for my next job—Chief of OSS in occupied Austria. Austria wasn't occupied yet but Kesselring was already negotiating the surrender of his armies in Northern Italy and further north Zhukov and Eisenhower were soon to join forces on the Elbe. It was almost all over now but the vodka drinking.

I hadn't been in Washington long when the end came.

Within twenty-four hours Congress and the press were yelling, "Bring the Boys Home." Perhaps it was inevitable, but I couldn't help feeling we were leaving the theater before the last act. A good many months earlier, we'd been asking the Russians on the European Advisory Commission: What plans have you when the shooting stops? Their silence had been ominous.

I caught the first plane I could for Austria. It was as good a place as any to find out the answer.

I found General Clark's headquarters in Florence preparing for the move to Vienna. There was only one small hitch. The Russians apparently weren't entirely sure they needed us in Vienna. They agreed they'd invited us but, they explained, they knew how much we liked our comforts, bathrooms, hot water, airfields, and so on, and most of these, they said, had been destroyed in the fighting. Wouldn't it be better if we just postponed our visit?

General Clark growled. The fact of the matter was, we did like our bathrooms and airfields but we weren't convinced they'd all been destroyed. So the French and British and ourselves suggested we send a little scouting party to survey what was left of Vienna's real estate. Reluctantly the Russians agreed, "in principle." They'd send a formal invitation for the party in a day or so. I was assigned to the scouting party as a "Russian Expert."

As usual with the Russians, there was a rather wide gap between the principle and the actual keys to the city. While we waited for our formal invitation, the Mission enjoyed the sights of Florence. Whenever you have to wait for Russians, there are few pleasanter places than Florence to do it in. But my waiting was abruptly interrupted.

I was having dinner one evening at the Hotel Excelsior when General Clark's aide called me to the phone to say that a plane would be ready for me at five a.m. the next morning to take me to Paris to see Harry Hopkins and Chip Bohlen who were returning from a visit to Moscow.

AFHQ in Italy always suffered from a slight claustrophobia because they said no one ever told them anything. Presumably my job was to buttonhole Hopkins and Bohlen in the Crillon Bar, and demand a full explanation of their recent activities. Five a.m. is a hell of a time to go anywhere—even Paris—but generals, I find, are often apt to overlook the habitual rising hours of their subordinates.

The plane was noisy but fast and in less than three hours we were over Orly Airfield. On the intercom system, I heard the pilot calling for landing instructions. The Control

Tower at Orly told us to land at Villa Coublai, an airfield many miles further from town.

"Only VIP's can land at Orly. Only VIP's. All others to Villa Coublai, to Villa Coublai. Over."

"I have a VIP on board" the pilot retorted looking back at me with a big wink. "I've a VIP aboard. Over."

"Whose your VIP? Over." The Control Tower asked suspiciously.

"Lt. Col. Thayer on board. Over," the pilot answered bravely.

"Nuts! He's no VIP. He's no VIP. Go to Villa Coublai. Go to Villa Coublai." There was no "over" this time. We were disposed of.

The pilot shrugged his shoulders. He'd done his best.

In the end it took longer to get from Villa Coublai to the Embassy than it had to get from Florence to Paris. And when I arrived I found Hopkins and Bohlen had already flown the coop. A telegram from Florence was waiting for me, saying that the Russians had finally gotten around to sending the invitation to come to Vienna. The Mission was scheduled to leave next morning. I was to turn around and come right back.

But the prospect of an evening in Paris isn't lightly given up, especially by an airplane crew. Also, I suspected the boys in Florence were a bit ahead of themselves if they thought the Russians were going to get out the red carpet and brush it off in twenty-four hours. So we did the usual rounds of Paris and next morning took off for Florence with mild headaches. Though we had failed in our mission, I could console myself with the thought that a hundred other Lieutenant Colonels were probably tearing around Europe at the moment on equally fruitless errands.

I got back to Florence in time for one final conference

with General Gruenther, Clark's Chief of Staff, to discuss our mission.

The job of the Special Mission, Gruenther said, was first to find a decent airfield for each of the Allies and second to inspect the city and report on what bathrooms, and so forth, were available.

The next day the "scouting party" set off in an impressive convoy for Vienna and got as far as the Russian zonal boundary, where we were told the Russians only wanted half as many people as we'd brought along. In a way you could hardly blame them. They expected a couple of Colonels and were confronted with three Generals plus enough "experts" to run the city three times over. But we dug our toes in and sent word we'd bring as many people as we liked.

When we returned to the zonal boundary next day, the Russians had forgotten their phobia for crowds and we were regally welcomed by a general from Tolbukhin's staff. As usual vodka and schnapps and champagne were broken out and it was a good two hours before we could wind up the international love feast and get on our way.

As our convoy, flying large American, British and French flags, entered the Austrian capital, the Viennese, who had not been expecting us, put on one of those demonstrative welcomes they alone can produce. They cheered, they yelled, they waved and crowded around us so much that you wondered whether perhaps there had been something wrong with the earlier Russian liberation.

It was obvious that the delirious welcome didn't exactly please our Russian host, though he laughed it off in a hearty way and quietly directed the convoy through back streets to a suburb where some houses had been requisitioned for us. As the Russians had expected only a fraction of the number of "scouts" that had turned up, we milled about for hours hunting for billets and beds. But eventually we were settled and sent a radio to Clark's headquarters in Florence that we'd arrived safely and wished he were there.

The next morning negotiations began. General Blagodatov, the Commandant of the city, represented the Russians; General Jack Winterton, the British; General Cherriere, the French; and General Flory, the Americans. We told the Russians we'd need some time to inspect all parts of the city and all the surrounding airports.

The Russians said they had one very nice airport that would do splendidly for all three western Allies. We could see the city and that airport. The inspection would only take a few days, they estimated, and they indicated quite clearly that within five days or a week their most welcome guests should get the hell out.

We repeated that we wanted to see *all* the airports in the vicinity, that we'd take as long as we liked to inspect the city and that we would reluctantly say goodbye to our hospitable hosts whenever we got good and ready.

The Russians looked a bit startled, whispered among themselves for a while, and then said that we shouldn't start by disagreeing but should get along with inspecting the city and the one airport. Then we could see about the rest. We said we'd like a clear agreement before we started.

For several hours we played a cozy game of cat and mouse, till General Flory said he would go back to his billet and stay there until our amiable Russian hosts had had time to appreciate the reasonableness of our offer. The Russians looked surprised when I translated this, and even more startled when Flory closed his briefcase, rose, shook hands affably and walked out. Winterton and Cherriere followed suit.

We drove back to our billet, wired Clark what we'd done and sat down to wait a bit nervously.

Late in the afternoon an amiable Russian general called to

explain that our wishes had been conveyed to Marshal Tolbukhin, who felt that we were going to waste our precious
time inspecting airfields we wouldn't consider using, but
that, of course, he had no objection to our seeing them if
we were so foolish as to insist. As for the length of our stay,
it was, of course, a pleasure to have us as long as we could
possibly afford to be away from home.

The next morning French, British and American survey
teams started scouring the city, precinct by precinct, noting
the damage, the number of hotels, barracks, storage facilities,
telephone installations and, of course, VIP villas for all the
VIP's that an occupation force requires. Other groups in-
spected several airports in the vicinity of town. The three
mission chiefs continued discussions with Soviet officials on
general conditions in Vienna. After our first meeting, all
was sweet cordiality though I noted that the mild-mannered
General Flory was listened to with considerably more defer-
ence since his original walk-out.

And, of course, there were parties. The Russians produced
a banquet, and the Western Allies returned the compliment.
The Russians filled their vodka glasses with water and the
Allied officers undertook to drink them under the table.
The results were a foregone conclusion.

We didn't have much time to devote to the Viennese,
though some of us found old friends and heard from them
all the horrors of the last months of the Allied bombings, of
the Nazi retreat, of the fighting in the streets, how the SS
themselves had bombarded and demolished most of the water front along the Danube. And, of course, of the rape and
pillage by Tolbukhin's Russian troops.

The Viennese were feeling very sorry for themselves. They
had lost their Opera House and most of their theaters. The
Prater was a shambles. The inner city was so piled with rub-

ble you could scarcely get through it. The roof of St. Stephen's Cathedral had collapsed and much of the interior had been burnt out. There were no cigarettes and very little food. And then, too, the Russians had stripped them of their watches! Not that it had ever made much difference to the Viennese what time of day it was, but the Red Soldiers didn't even know how to wind them.

On top of it all they had their Hungarian relatives. One old Viennese minor aristocrat shook his head sadly. "Our Hungarian relations will never learn. When Russians threatened to overrun them in the last war, they all flocked to Vienna. They always do. And what did they bring with them? Nothing but case after case of their favorite wines. They sat around the Grand Hotel and the Bristol and Sacher's Hotel and played cards till their wine and money gave out and then they came to their Austrian cousins and camped on us until the war was over. Time and again we told them, 'Next time leave your damn wines at home. Let the Russians drink it. But bring your jewelry, your silver, something you can sell and live off of till you can get back home.'"

The old count sighed. "But do you think those damned cousins remembered? The fools turned up as we'd expected, when the Russians got close to Budapest, and what do you suppose they brought this time? Their race horses! They loaded their farm carts with their children, and grain for the thoroughbreds and rode their horses right to Vienna. What they thought anyone could do with a race horse in Vienna in the middle of all the bombing, God knows. When I looked out the window of my little house and saw all my cousins from Budapest, all fourteen, milling around in the street on a herd of tired thoroughbreds, I cried. Hungarians will never learn! And what do you suppose they did with their jewelry? They 'hid' it, they said, in their houses. So the houses are wrecked, the jewelry's gone and all they have are those damned race horses!"

What the Russians had to say about the Viennese was not much better. "Lazy, good-for-nothing, philosophizing, sloppy sentimentalists. Why, they won't even clean up the city. They say they haven't got enough bread or coal to make it worth while to work. All they do is cry about their damned old Opera House you Americans bombed. We can't make them do anything. They simply sip the wine and beer they hid from our soldiers and talk about the good old days.

"And their so-called art! Have you seen it? Why, they make statues of soldiers without clothes on. And paint nude women—all circles and bumps with purple bodies! That's not the kind of art we have in Moscow."

Obviously the good people of Vienna had the Russians thoroughly bewildered—and still do.

Eventually the survey teams were through. Vienna had been inventoried and appraised precinct by precinct, street by street, house by house, as it had never been before. The airfields had been examined, measured and tested by the air experts. The problems of joint occupation had been thoroughly discussed by the mission heads. Ten days had elapsed since our arrival. Marshal Tolbukhin's staff gave us another banquet, and the convoy moved off through the Alps back to Florence where we reported our findings to General Clark. Now the "higher levels" could parcel out the city, and then the Allied troops could take over the joint occupation.

I was released and told to go back to the OSS. A few days later I arrived in Salzburg to take over the OSS Mission for Austria.

The chief activity of the Mission when I got there seemed to be concerned with catching Nazis. When Hitler's house

began to tumble down, many of the bigger and wickeder
Nazi fish hustled off to the Tyrol where it was rumored Hitler was going to make a glorious Wagnerian last stand in the
so-called Alpine Redoubt. For months before the war ended,
innumerable Allied intelligence services had been making
statements about the Redoubt: how it was fortified, stocked,
manned, provisioned. After the war each intelligence agency
found all the necessary evidence to prove whatever its view
of the Redoubt had been before and everyone was happy.
But the fact remains that the Redoubt was as mythical as
Wagner's operas, and so was the last stand.

Nevertheless, many of Hitler's henchmen were quite as
badly fooled as the Allied Intelligence Agencies, and they
flocked to the Tyrol with their families and their loot and their
archives. The area was excellent to hide in and perhaps too,
they figured, if there wasn't a last stand, at least they could
"just fade away" in the wild, craggy mountains.

Our job was to run them down. I never understood how
our people did it, but they succeeded in rounding up all
sorts of odd characters and putting them in prison cages.
They seemed to enjoy doing it too and I suspected they made
rather a game of it, with a special score for each type of
character they caught: ten points for a *gauleiter;* eight points
for an SS *obersturmbahnfuhrer;* five for a general and finally
one point for just a plain common Party functionary.

One of the highest scorers was Captain Rudolph Von Ripper. Ripper was an Austrian-born artist who had come to
America, become a citizen and had fought throughout the
Italian campaign in one strange capacity after another. He
was well up in the hierarchy of screwballs in many respects.
His favorite gambit was to slip behind enemy lines on a
dark night and strike up conversations with any German
soldiers he happened to meet as he sauntered down the road
from one German position to another.

In Salzburg, Ripper, a native of the area, was uncanny in his ability to smell out *gauleiters* and other high ranking Nazis. His methods, I suspected, were hardly orthodox so I never looked into them too carefully. But his results were excellent. And he didn't concentrate on mere human flesh. Occasionally his hauls included more substantial stuff.

One day Ripper appeared in my office dressed not as a Captain in the U.S. Army, but like a Tyrolean yodler from the White Horse Inn. On his head was a ridiculous little green hat with the beard of chamois sticking out of its band like a shaving brush. The rest of his get-up included a short grey jacket with green piping and bone buttons, a pair of filthy black *lederhosen,* white knit stockings held up by fancy green garters, and a pair of old ski boots.

The costume seemed just a little more irregular than necessary and I started to bawl him out. Then I noticed he was soaked to the skin and carrying a large bag that was dripping puddles of water on the floor.

"Captain, what the hell do you think you're up to? You may be able to get away with that sort of nightclub costume up in the hills, but when you come to the office . . . And what the devil's the idea of coming in here dripping like a wet rag? Go to your quarters and. . . ."

Grinning toothily, Rip paid no attention to my tirade and proceeded to dump the sopping sack onto my desk.

"But Colonel, I just found something. . . ."

"Found something! You're always finding things. Won't it keep till you've changed into a dry uniform? What is it anyway that it won't keep? A rare orchid from the upper reaches of the Alps?"

"No, Colonel. Only about a million pounds sterling. I haven't counted it all yet."

Ripper explained "someone" had told him that just before the German surrender, a suspicious looking truck with a Berlin license plate had arrived under heavy guard in the neighborhood of Salzburg. After wandering around for several days, it had been seen one night parked on a bridge over the Enns River. Its driver and guards seemed to be throwing stuff into the river. That was a good enough tip for Rip. He'd fetched a couple of boats, some grappling hooks and a few hundred feet of rope and carted them over to the bridge. The Enns River at that point is a fairly shallow but fast flowing mountain stream. The chief difficulty, however, was that the river was the boundary between the Russian and American zones, and Russian guards were as thick as fleas on the opposite bank.

Rip was having no truck with the Russians and he certainly wasn't going to go shares with them on any loot he might salvage from the river. So the operation had to be controlled from our bank with the necessary precautions against being carried over to the other bank by the current where the Russians would undoubtedly have seized the whole kit and caboodle. Rip admitted he was no boatman, but somehow after hours of floundering about in the icy river under the curious eyes of the Russian sentries, he managed to hook up from the bottom several sacks, each with a dozen or so thick packets of five pound notes.

We telegraphed our London office that same day and by the next afternoon a flock of British bank officials and Scotland Yard agents were on the scene. Ever since the war had started, they'd been plagued all over the world by the counterfeit notes which the Germans had made so well as to defy detection except by experts. When the war ended they were terrified, not only lest the remaining stocks get into circulation, but that the plates, so beautifully made, would fall into the hands of the Russians or a similar organization. For weeks they continued to drag the river under the Russians' noses but, so far as I know, the plates have never shown up. Maybe the Russians got them after all.

I got involved in a manhunt only once and managed to throw not only the OSS but the CIC and several other agencies into a first class confusion until we found our man. But my quarry was not a gauleiter or an SS butcher—just an old friend who happened to be a captain in the German Army.

I'd known Jonny von Herwarth since 1934 in Moscow. He was one of the seeded players in the favorite Moscow game of guessing what the Russians were going to do next, and he could spend hours arguing with anyone who would argue back about the meaning of this decree or that speech. Why was Molotov's picture closer to Stalin's than Kalinin's? What had happened to Mikoyan's standing since he became Commissar for Food? How much of a fake was the "Stalin Constitution"? Why had the Kremlin suddenly forbidden abortions?

Jonny had always been a staunch German. But like his boss, Count Schulenburg, the German Ambassador, he made no bones about the fact that he considered Hitler a catastrophe not only for Germany's neighbors but for Germany herself. When, as a result of Hitler's and Ribbentrop's diplomacy, Germany found herself allied to Russia and at war with western Europe, Jonny quit his job in the Foreign Service in protest and joined up with a German cavalry regiment. Once or twice we caught a glimpse of him when he came back to Moscow on leave but when Germany attacked Russia we lost track of him. We suspected that because of his knowledge of Russian and Russia he'd be somewhere on the Russian front and once or twice we got news of him through neutrals. We heard he was working with General Koestring, for many years the German military attaché in Moscow, later Inspector General for all "volunteers" (Russians) in the German Army. We also heard Jonny was in the Caucasus and then in the Balkans.

Once when MacLean and I were in Belgrade, Tito had told us that a German directive had been captured according to which the heads of the Allied Missions to Tito were to be shot on sight as spies. We were both very pleased by this recognition and boasted of it proudly. Then a few weeks later Tito told us his Partisans had captured an amendment to the directive. MacLean and myself were not to be shot after all. On the contrary we were to be treated as VIP-POW's and forwarded to Higher Headquarters.

"What," asked Tito, "does this mean?"

MacLean looked at me. I looked at MacLean. We both felt a bit crestfallen.

Then MacLean had an inspiration.

"Jonny must be around."

"Who's Jonny?" Tito asked and we explained he was a friend, but unfortunately on the wrong side of the front. Tito seemed satisfied, and we more or less forgot about the matter as the chances of getting captured by the Germans became more remote.

By the time we got to Salzburg, I'd pretty well given up hope of ever seeing Jonny again. He must have been on the Russian front, I thought, and if captured, I knew it would be a long time before he'd be seen again this side of Siberia.

Then one day the Political Advisor's Office phoned me.

"Do you know a German officer called Bittenfeld?" they asked.

The name rang a very faint bell.

"Bittenfeld? Hasn't he got another name too?"

"Yes, he calls himself Herwarth von Bittenfeld."

"Why, that's Jonny Herwarth. Of course I know him."

"Well, he came in here ten minutes ago and he gave your name among other American diplomats he knew."

"Get the CIC to arrest him and send him over to me at once," I told them.

"He's not here any more. We figured you didn't want to be pestered, so we didn't let on you were right here."

I called the CIC in Salzburg and told them that there was a German Army Officer running around loose in Salzburg whom I wanted very badly.

Besides the fact that he was an old friend, I wanted Jonny for another and much more important reason. As a Russian expert, his observations on the Russian front and in Russia would be invaluable. Aside from a few staged trips to the front for our military attachés in Moscow and what I and perhaps a handful of escaping POW's had seen in the Balkans, none of us had as yet any inkling of what had really happened on the Russian front since June 22, 1941, except for the rather sketchy and not altogether reliable reports of the Russians themselves. If we could find Jonny, there were a lot of questions he could answer, and from my experience with him before the war I was sure those answers would not only be reliable but expert. For Jonny was not only a convinced anti-Nazi. He knew Russia as few other foreigners knew it.

When I'd explained all this to the CIC they agreed to assign every agent they could spare to looking for Jonny. But they explained it wasn't going to be easy. Austria was swarming with ex-soldiers and officers who'd made their way individually from the Balkans and Italy looking for a demobilization camp where they could be processed and sent home without too much delay. Most of the demobilization camps were so jammed with units which had surrendered in a body that they weren't at all anxious to accept these strays that straggled in one by one. But anyway CIC said they'd try. From the OSS mission everyone who could walk was told to look for Jonny. We combed Salzburg. We searched the neighboring villages. We searched the demobilization camps. But no Jonny. The CIC said it was hopeless but I persuaded them to keep trying. Our own men were very unhappy at the interruption of the game of "Hunt the Gauleiter" but I did my best to egg them on. Ten days went by without a sign of the missing German Captain.

One rainy morning I was driving to Salzburg from the OSS billet in the suburbs. We'd gone about a hundred yards when I caught sight of a hunched-up, miserable-looking German officer standing at the gate of the schloss next to ours.

It was Jonny all right. I called to the driver to stop and in violation of every rule of military etiquette and the anti-fraternization directive, clapped my arm around his shoulder.

"Ouch," screamed Jonny. "I've got terrible lumbago."

He was very hungry too. So I took him at once to our clinic where the doctor strapped up his back and gave him some food. Jonny in the meantime explained that when the surrender came he'd been in Kitzbühel where Pussi, his wife, had a little chalet. When the Americans arrived, he'd been befriended by an American Signal Corps Captain who made him his interpreter and brought him to Salzburg. Then the Signal Corps Detachment had been temporarily sent elsewhere and Jonny was left stranded in Salzburg where he found to his dismay that his food ration cards from Kitzbühel were no good. So for three days he'd gone hungry, while he hung about the schloss next door waiting for his Signal Corps Captain to come back.

I sent word to Ashcan, the interrogation center for high German officials, and told them I had Jonny. "Interrogate him yourself," they replied. Then I got him demobilized. For three weeks Jonny stayed with me while I swamped him with questions. I even asked him about those directives Tito had shown us.

Jonny smiled modestly.

"I just happened to see that first order that you were to be shot. I didn't really think they'd catch either you or Fitzroy MacLean but just to be on the safe side I got General Koe-string to amend the order. After all, if things had turned out differently, I wouldn't have wanted to miss the chance of interrogating you."

Jonny's story: what happened to Hitler in Russia

TWELVE

"no foreigner is going to put his pig's snout in our garden" was Stalin's delicate way of warning his neighbors not to invade Russia in the thirties. At that time Jonny and I were serving as secretaries of Embassy in Moscow—he of the German, I in the American—and we duly dispatched to the Wilhelmstrasse and the State Department lengthy telegrams transmitting Stalin's comment as well as innumerable predictions produced by *Pravda* and *Izvestija* as to what the Soviet people would do to any pig that did get its snout under the Soviet Union's gate. Every Soviet man, woman and child, said *Pravda*, would rise in fury to hurl out the intruder. Not only

Pravda said it, but the Soviet radio, film industry, writers' union, and theater; even the ballet produced pilot models of this great national uprising.

Jonny had been a little sceptical about the accuracy of these prognostications and so had I, especially after a whole village full of peasants near Moscow had told me back in 1941 that if they had some rifles they'd seize the Kremlin and replace its occupants with Hitler's men. When Jonny resigned from the German Foreign Service in protest against Hitler's habit of making war, he started in as a lieutenant in one of Germany's last cavalry regiments. The regiment had been allowed to keep its horses because a few of Hitler's generals knew what Russian roads are like and decided horse cavalry was the only practical way of getting around fast. Consequently on June 22, 1941, when Hitler did invade Stalin's garden, Jonny found himself one of the advance whiskers on the Nazi pig's snout.

Jonny had hardly crossed the frontier that tragic Sunday morning when he began to meet hordes of Russian soldiers politely requesting to be counted out of the contest. "We could hardly make a reconnaissance," he told me, "because I kept having to detach my men to escort the surrendering Russians to the POW cages. Even though I kept the ratio to one German private for every 1000 POW's we'd usually be out of men before we'd gone ten miles."

"Were you surprised?" I asked.

"Not exactly," Jonny answered laconically. "But I was once, on that first Sunday."

Among the Russian soldiers who gave themselves up that day to Jonny's patrol was an officer with captain's insignia on his blouse and the red piping of Soviet Artillery. When he discovered Jonny could speak Russian he pushed forward and grabbed the bridle of Jonny's horse.

"Quick, tell me where the German artillery is," he shouted.

Jonny pointed out he was a prisoner of war and the location of the German artillery was not only none of his damned business, but also something that wasn't going to make much difference to him from then on out.

"But damn it, Comrade Enemy," the Russian persisted shaking the bridle impatiently. "I've got to find your artillery fire control post at once. They're firing a good thousand meters short of our battery and I've got to tell them to raise their range and shift right four points."

"That," Jonny admitted, "did surprise me a little."

A day or so later, Jonny galloped into a village just evacuated by the Reds. The streets were lined with peasants shouting and waving gleefully. A flight of German fighter bombers roared overhead to be met by a squadron of Russian planes. In the battle that followed all the Russian planes were knocked down. As each crashed to the ground in flames the Russian villagers screamed for joy and clapped their hands. "Soon Stalin will be kaput," they shouted.

"But he wasn't," Jonny added as a second thought.

"For those first few months while they fell back there was no fight in the Red Army. Whenever they dug in they were first class. Afterwards when they were advancing they were good. But when they were retreating they just sat down in the ditches and gave up."

I had been in Moscow during those months. Until then Hitler had whipped everything he'd come up against: Austria, Czechoslovakia, Poland, Denmark and Norway, the Low Countries, and finally France. I remembered how we sat gloomily around the radio in Moscow and hoped for some miracle to stop Hitler.

"But you did get stopped," I reminded Jonny, "and eventually got licked. Why?"

"It was a number of things: Winter, of course, was the worst. Hitler had refused to fit out the troops with winter clothing. He said it would all be over before they'd need them—just like Napoleon and just as wrong. Koestring warned him. The General Staff warned him but he never listened."

Then came the new Soviet Armies Stalin had been training behind the Volga. They were the ones that threw the Germans back from Moscow.

"But I'm inclined to think the biggest factor was political: the way we treated the population and the prisoners we captured. When we first marched into Russia, the peasants met us literally with bread and salt. The more intelligent Russians in the captured towns began to talk about 'Restoring the Dignity of Man.' One thing they all wanted was to break up the Collective Farms. Where the German Army was in control, we tried to persuade the peasants to go ahead and collect the grain individually and then divide it up fairly. It was what they wanted but it was wasteful, and what Hitler wanted was grain. So he gave orders to keep the Collective Farms intact. Later in some places we managed to reorganize the Collectives into free cooperatives and that worked pretty well, especially in the Caucasus. Among the Armenian settlements along the Black Sea we did well too. They liked Koestring because he was very dark and had a great beak of a nose. They'd point at him and say "Everything's o.k. now. One of our boys is a German General already!"

"But how did you run the towns and villages when the whole Soviet bureaucratic machinery collapsed?" I asked.

"That was easy as long as Hitler didn't interfere. We just told the town to elect its own council and get going. They did and it worked. But we did all that against Hitler's orders. As the Army moved on, the Reichs Commissars of the German Civil Administration of the Eastern Area changed that. Koch, the Reichs Commissar for the Ukraine, for instance, hadn't the vaguest idea about Russia when he was appointed. He made the peasants keep their Collectives. He didn't allow the Ukrainians or Russians to do anything but physical work. He began transporting the peasants to Germany to work in the factories. 'East-workers' we called them. At first he asked for volunteers. The first who volunteered he put in cattle cars and shipped west to Germany where they were kept in barbed-wire camps on half rations. Naturally, a few escaped and came back and told what was going on. Then there were no more volunteers. So Koch rounded them up by force, and when they complained he put them in jail and even shot a few."

The Germans even succeeded in making an enemy of their greatest potential ally, the Church. When they first came, everyone flocked to church again for the first time since the Revolution. And it wasn't just to please the Germans. They were still deeply religious.

"I remember in one village," Jonny told me, "some Russian counter artillery had set fire to the straw thatched huts and the wind blew flames toward the rest of the village. A young Russian with an ikon in his hands climbed on a roof that wasn't burning yet and started to pray aloud to God to change the wind. Our soldiers began to laugh at him, but I told them to shut up. Was there any other way but a change of wind to prevent the entire village from burning? And who but God could change it?"

As though they were looking for ways to make it hard for themselves, the Germans who had to collect East-workers had the bright idea of rounding up villagers when they left church each Sunday and shipping them off in cattle cars to Germany. Soon enough, the Russians decided church-going wasn't as healthy as they'd hoped.

"But what we did to the Russian prisoners was the top of insanity as well as criminality," Jonny said bitterly. "You can't say Hitler ordered that they be starved to death. I don't think the Army would have obeyed him. He simply refused to have any food assigned to the feeding of prisoners. The result was that in the first months probably more than a million starved to death in their barbed-wire cages. Our Generals protested to Hitler. But it didn't do any good. He hadn't paid any attention to them since the fall of France."

"Then what we read in *Pravda* and *Izvestiya* in those days was more or less true," I interrupted.

"Of course it was true—too damned true! They may have exaggerated a little about individual atrocities by the troops. Our troops behaved pretty well. But it didn't take long for the Russians to know they were being sold from one form of slavery to another. And I guess they figured they were used to their old slave driver. So they started to fight for him— six months late, but not too late. And that's how Germany lost the war in the East," Jonny concluded with a grim smile.

In 1942 Jonny had gone to work with his old chief General Koestring, whose job it was to look after the Russian volunteers fighting for Germany. There were two kinds of volunteers. Some were immediately put to work by their captors at the front, first in menial jobs and later, as the German divisions began to dwindle, in more important jobs. As Jonny put it, "Every Fritz had his Ivan to help him. When Fritz got wounded, Ivan took over the gun."

Other volunteers were organized into battalions made up exclusively of Russians with German instructors. That was the so-called Vlassov Army. In all there were about 700,-000 Russians in the German Army by the time the surrender came, including the two famous Cossack divisions in Yugoslavia that had caused Arso so much trouble. But Hitler was always blocking Koestring's efforts to use these units.

"Hitler said we could use their sweat," Jonny said, "but not their blood. If they spilt their blood, he figured, they might try to cash in on it later when he started colonizing the conquered territories.

"Those Russians were marvelous fighters too. They worked harder, ate less, slept less and took far better care of their equipment than our own troops. For instance, the German General Army Group, North, on the retreat from Leningrad, published an order after the withdrawal saying that 'thanks to the loyalty and courage of the 'Volunteers' we were able to bring back all our equipment and heavy weapons.' Later in 1944 when some divisions were transferred from the Eastern Front to the West Wall in France, they were told at first they couldn't bring their Ivans with them. But the Division Commanders protested and demanded two Fritzes for every Ivan left behind. The High Command was afraid to tell that to Hitler and in the end just closed their eyes to the Ivans. When the breakthrough came and troops began to desert, the German M.P.'s had a hell of a time because whenever they questioned a suspected German deserter, he'd just answer "Nicht Verstehen" pretending to be a Russian.

"But our real failure was the failure to provide them with a political ideal—a goal to fight for. Hitler had forbidden it. You can't ask a body of troops like that to fight unless you promise them something at the end of the battle. Don't forget that, if you're ever unlucky enough to be in the same position. You must give them the political ideal—or allow them to create their own. That's even better."

Jonny sighed, "Anyway it was a failure—a terrible failure. I don't know if we could ever really have conquered Russia but if Hitler had not been so stupid at least we might have destroyed Stalin." There was a long silence.

"The only way we might have done it was to get rid of

Hitler himself," Jonny said at last, "and we failed there too —by the thickness of a table leg."

During the war, news of the July 20 plot had trickled through the lines but the details hadn't become known. In 1942, Jonny told me, he'd met Count Claus Stauffenberg, a cousin of his wife, and they talked as usual about Hitler. At that time they discussed whether Hitler was solely to blame or whether his lieutenants, Goering, Himmler, Goebbels, and the rest were the real villains. In the summer of 1943 Captain Kuhn, a friend of Stauffenberg, had looked up Jonny again in East Prussia. This time the discussion was more concrete.

"Are you just a Kibitzer?" Kuhn asked. "Or are you ready to do something about it? Think it over and when you've decided let me know." Kuhn went away.

"I knew what he meant," Jonny told me. "It was a ghastly decision to make. It was one thing to curse Hitler and hate him but to kill him was something else again. You've never been asked to help prepare a murder and you probably won't understand my feelings. I cursed my own foolish talk that got me into the dilemma. I thought of asking to go back to my regiment on the Eastern Front. But I couldn't avoid a decision that way or any other. The real question I had to face was whether God Himself would allow even such a killing. I never really answered the question. I got around it by saying: If Hitler must be killed it is simply my fate for better or worse to help in the killing. So in the end I got in touch with Kuhn and said I'd go along."

"How long did it take you, Jonny?" I asked.

"Twenty-four hours about—the longest and most disagreeable twenty-four hours I've ever spent."

Today we know the conspiracy to kill Hitler involved hundreds of Germans, almost all of whom were executed after the 20th of July attempt failed. They included politicians of the left and right, intellectual and religious leaders, and a group of Army Officers under Stauffenberg and General Beck. It was this last group on whom everyone relied for the actual killing. The others were to prepare the political measures to take over afterwards. Both jobs were equally dangerous. At the time Jonny only knew a handful of his fellow conspirators for, like all good undergrounds, the opposition was divided into cells.

"Our first idea was to get Himmler and Goering along with Hitler. The plan called for a practice maneuver, like a boat-drill, designed to save the High Brass from a simulated enemy paratroop raid on Supreme Headquarters. In the course of the drill we would herd Hitler, Himmler and Goering into a shelter and then blow them up. We prepared sheafs of orders which were to have been sent out when Hitler and his boys had been killed. Naturally these orders contained lots of names of reliable anti-Nazis most of whom were in the conspiracy. We'd also got hold of a bomb of British make which we planned to use. It seems funny that with a dozen or more generals in the plot we couldn't risk taking our own high explosive from the Ordnance supplies. We had to rely on an enemy-made bomb. We kept the bomb under the bed of one of the conspirators, General Stieff. But then General Stieff was sent on leave and we were afraid his orderly might find the bomb so we went out into the woods one night and buried both the orders and the bomb in two separate holes.

"Unfortunately, however, someone must have been watching us because that night the M.P.'s came with police dogs and searched the woods and found the bomb, but not the orders. Just as I thought the jig was up, the dogs followed a false scent that lead not to our office but to the hut of the Quartermaster General. The General was a terribly bad tempered old man. We always called him 'Nero'. When he was

waked up by a lot of police dogs milling around in his bedroom he raised such hell that the M.P.'s ran away in confusion. But they did report finding the bomb to their Chief,
Colonel Schräder. He was a good anti-Nazi and knew something of what we were up to but of course he had no idea that
the bomb was ours. So we went to tell him and try to persuade him to quash the investigation."

Jonny laughed cheerfully as he described the little mission which meant life or death to him and his fellow conspirators.

"When we got Schäder alone and explained that it was
our bomb I thought he was going to faint. His eyes almost
popped out of his head, his hands began to tremble and the
sweat started rolling off his big bald head. But I managed
to calm him down and after a little arguing he agreed to
stop the investigation.

"That was the end of that failure," Jonny concluded sar-
donically. "Schräder and 'Nero' were both killed after the
20th of July.

"Eventually one of Stauffenberg's men found a second
bomb and a new plan to blow up Hitler in Berchtesgaden
was worked out. It was all set for the 13th of July and I reported to Berchtesgaden with some fake orders the night before to be on hand in case they needed me. But something
went wrong again and the attempt was postponed."

By this time Himmler and the SS had got wind that things
were stirring among the plotters. Nerves were getting a bit
taut and the conspirators realized they had no more time to
lose. So Stauffenberg decided that come hell or high water,
he'd have to make a final attempt on the 20th when a regular staff meeting was to take place with Hitler at his Headquarters in East Prussia. He quickly made preparations for
reliable troops to take over Berlin and Supreme Headquarters in East Prussia. Jonny was sent to Kesselring's Headquar-

ters in Italy to alert the plotters there. After Jonny had carried out his assignment he started back for Potsdam where Stauffenberg had ordered him to be by the 18th—two days before "X" day.

But at this point the U.S. Airforce intervened. They managed to dominate the air over northern Italy so thoroughly that all German planes were grounded. In a panic, Jonny managed to get a train as far as Verona. North of Verona the railroad had been put out of commission by bombing. He hooked a ride on a truck as far as the Brenner Pass. But the Pass too had taken such a plastering from the Airforce that it was closed. Finally on the night of the 20th Jonny had managed to get as far as Berchtesgaden. There to his horror he learned not only that the plot had failed but that Stauffenberg and most of his fellow conspirators were under arrest.

Realizing that this time the jig was really up, Jonny went to nearby Kitzbühel in the Austrian Alps where his wife was living. Convinced that his role in the plot had become known, he sat down and waited for the Gestapo to fetch him. As the hours passed and they didn't come he tried to figure out how to escape. Should he go up into the mountains and hide? Should he go to Yugoslavia and try to get through to Fitzroy MacLean or myself? Or should he try to bluff it through? Either of the first two moves would arouse suspicion and almost certainly result in reprisals against his wife and little daughter, Alexei. He chose the third alternative and with great misgiving said goodbye to his family and set out for Potsdam where he arrived on the 23rd. By this time dozens of suspected conspirators had already been arrested and more were being picked up every hour.

Jonny went straight to his office, sat down at his desk and tried to act as though nothing had happened. Then his eye fell on a chit that had been left on his blotter by his secretary. It was dated the 18th and had obviously been lying there for five days:

"Please call Colonel Stauffenberg's ADC urgently as soon as you come in."

"For a moment my heart stopped beating," Jonny said. "How could that have lain there for five days without any-one reading it? Stauffenberg and his Aide had been shot on the evening of the 20th. I didn't know what to do. I got up from my desk and with my knees wobbling every which way I went over to my locker, pulled out a flask of brandy and had three quick shots. Then I took the paper, tore it into little scraps and flushed it down the toilet.

"Just then a friend of mine walked in.

" 'You're looking a little pale, Jonny,' he told me. He must have suspected why. Anyway he took me to his quar-ters, opened another bottle of cognac, and in a half an hour I was roaring drunk and feeling fine.

"Then I went to my boss, General Koestring. He took one look at me and said, 'Captain, get the hell out of Berlin and quick.' He'd never been in on the plot but he'd sus-pected for a long time I was mixed up in it. He'd made some half-hearted attempts to warn me. 'You're always in trouble, Jonny,' he'd say. But in the end he always gave me all the time I needed and fake travel orders so that I could go about my business for Stauffenberg.

"So when he told me to go away, I said I wouldn't leave without him. Some of those fake orders might turn up and he'd be in the soup. In the end we decided to make an in-spection tour of the Russian volunteers in Yugoslavia. When we got to Belgrade the Gestapo was still making arrests but soon they stopped. I guess Hitler decided he'd given us enough of a blood bath and besides he wanted Ger-many to forget about the conspiracy. Such things are always a little disagreeable for dictators—even when they fail."

i was

cooking my breakfast over an open camp fire, high up in the Austrian Alps when a motorcycle messenger roared up the steep path to the shooting hut. He handed me a letter telling me to be at General Gruenther's quarters at ten o'clock, prepared to go to Vienna. I'd been up since 2 a.m. shooting chamois and the prospect of a long ride to Vienna wasn't precisely my idea of the way to spend a hot summer Sunday in Austria. But orders were orders. I packed up and in a few minutes was on my way.

The mountain road from Gastein to Salzburg is narrow, steep and very windy. As I was approaching one sharp turn, a ten-ton army truck coming in the opposite direction, roared around the curve thoroughly out of control. The driver made a frantic effort to keep his vehicle on the road, but he didn't have a prayer and a moment later the truck seemed to sail majestically off among the trees into a deep ravine. By the time I'd clambered down the embankment, the truck had come to rest half way down the slope with its wheels in the air. I hunted high and low around the wreckage for the driver's body, but there wasn't a sign of it. Suddenly I heard a grunt from the bottom of the ravine where a mountain stream cut through a sunlit patch of grass. There, among the wild flowers, sat a G.I. He looked a little dazed.

"Geez," he said, "I sure picked a pretty spot. Or is this Heaven?" I left him to worry about getting his truck out and hurried on to General Gruenther's.

A couple of hours later we were speeding toward Vienna in a long cavalcade of star-spangled staff cars led by three motorcycle escorts, their sirens screaming madly as we wove recklessly in and out of the traffic. I thought of the upset G.I. and wished I was sitting peacefully beside him among the Edelweiss.

Late in the afternoon we reached Soviet Headquarters in Vienna and without any preliminary "little vodkas" we set to work ironing out the remaining obstacles to the joint occupation of Vienna. Who was to feed the starving Viennese? Who was to police the city? What kinds of passes would Allied troops have to carry? And a dozen more "details."

At 11 p.m. we were still at it when General Petrov, the Russian, suggested a break for supper. In an adjoining room we found a table loaded with food and drink. Realizing we had plenty of details still to iron out, I filled my vodka glass with water, as Marshal Tolbukhin had taught me, and joined the toast-drinking with gusto, safe in the knowledge that I had a bottle of benzedrine in my pocket in case I needed some extra energy.

By the time we sat down to work again my fellow interpreters, after a few glasses of vodka, were as lively as young pups. Just to keep up I munched a half a benzedrine tablet. A half hour later the Russian interpreter began to doze. Soon the Frenchman was looking a bit sleepy. Finally the Englishman, a cousin of mine incidentally, was nodding. I swallowed the second half of the benzedrine tablet and took over for Petrov's interpreter. When the Frenchman's head dropped on his chest, I took another half a tablet and added French to my translations. Ten minutes later even my young English cousin started napping.

The subject under discussion was how many troops each of the Allies planned to quarter in Vienna.

"Troops," "troupes," "truppen," were repeated a dozen times in English, French and German. Wearily I translated into Russian, "Truppi." After several minutes General Petrov interrupted:

"I appreciate that the Colonel is tired but would he mind not marching so many *truppi* (Russian for *corpses*) around Vienna and replace them with *voiska* (troops)."

I apologized for the slip and we went on.

Two o'clock came and went. I'd been on the go for twenty-four hours already and had to come down the stretch translating for four tired short-tempered generals in three languages. I swallowed another benzedrine tablet.

It was nearly three o'clock when Petrov interrupted the discussions.

"I think it is time for the generals to go to bed. However, the apparatus," he added looking at me, "should continue to work and draft a protocol of our agreements to be signed when awake."

"Excuse me, General," I apologized, "I don't mind too much staying up the rest of the night but do you have to call me an 'apparatus'?"

General Petrov smiled and nodded appreciatively.

"I stand corrected," he said, "I suggest the generals go to bed and the Colonel here will get the papers in order for signature in the morning."

When the generals had left, I roused my French and British colleagues (the Russian was still deep in sleep), rousted out some stenographers from their beds and by six a.m. the protocols were ready for signature. All we had to do was agree the texts in the various languages. That required the initials of the Soviet interpreter. So we propped the sleepy Russian in a chair and held an English text in front of him while my English cousin read the Russian text to him as fast as he could. Each time the Russian's head began to nod I shook him till he came to. When Cousin Alec was done we asked the Russian if he agreed. He nodded sleepily. We put a pen in his hands. He scribbled some initials and the job was done. A little more benzedrine, a cup of coffee, a shave and I was ready to go on.

The generals reappeared, sleepy and out of sorts, around seven in the morning, signed the protocols, discussed a few more disagreed topics for an hour or two and the conference was over.

Once back in Salzburg the tireless General Gruenther set us to work preparing a detailed report of the trip. Thanks to a few more nibbles of benzedrine I managed to get through that. When it was all done Gruenther slapped me hard on the back. "And now," he said, "the apparatus can go to bed, too." Forty-eight strenuous hours after I'd crawled out of bed to shoot a chamois, I crawled into another bed back in Salzburg and slept around the clock.

But apparently, the Russians still weren't quite ready for us to come to Vienna. There were a number of additional "details" they wouldn't agree on. So General Gruenther took me back to Vienna to work them out. This time we dealt with Colonel General Zheltov, my old acquaintance from Hungarian days. The talks dragged on for several days without much progress. Zheltov was primarily a Communist Party official and only incidentally in the uniform of a Colonel General. So he was a good bit more difficult to handle than the generals' general we'd been dealing with. Eventually, as the deadlock continued, Gruenther flew back to see General Clark in Salzburg leaving me behind in Vienna. The next day a telegram from Clark crackled through the ether:

"Go see Zheltov and tell him for me that if he keeps on procrastinating, I shall ask President Truman to complain to Stalin."

I read the cable and smiled. It wasn't exactly protocol for a lieutenant colonel to tell a colonel general where to get off even as a proxy, but Clark was obviously mad and had no time for protocol.

So I trotted over to the Grand Hotel where Zheltov had his headquarters.

I said I had an important message from General Clark for Zheltov. I was immediately shown into a large tapestry-hung salon in the far corner of which Zheltov was sitting at a very ornate flat topped desk. I walked up to the desk, saluted as snappily as I could. Zheltov returned the salute and asked me what I wanted.

Speaking very slowly, I repeated General Clark's message. Zheltov didn't explode. He fissioned.

"What in the name of God do you mean bringing me a message like that?"

"Orders, sir," I replied. "Orders from General Clark."

"You, a mere lieutenant colonel, telling me, a colonel general," he spluttered. "I won't accept that message from you! No, I won't!" Zheltov got up from his chair, stamped up and down the ornate salon at a great rate. "You shall write down what you have said to me." He pulled a chair out from the conference table in the middle of the room, threw a pad and pencil in front of it and turned on me.

"Sit down and write out what you just said."

I smiled sweetly but didn't move.

"I'm ordering you, Colonel." The General was trembling with rage. I remained standing.

"I'll repeat it for you," I suggested, "and you can write it down. I was told to tell you, not write you."

Zheltov's voice dropped to a bad imitation of restraint. He spoke very slowly and emphatically:

"Colonel, as your superior Allied General, I order you to sit down and write that message down." I didn't budge.

"Colonel, don't you obey orders?"

"Always, sir—when the orders come through the proper channels."

Zheltov didn't answer at once. Still trembling he sat down at his desk and after a long pause repeated, "I won't accept the message." He picked up some papers and began to read to himself.

"Have you any reply for General Clark, sir?"

Zheltov stiffened but said nothing.

"Then if that is all, sir. . . . ?" Still no reply.

I threw out a great big salute which he ignored, took a step to the rear, did an about-face and walked out. (Some of the little things you learn at West Point come in very useful on rare occasions.)

I reported by radio that Clark's message had been delivered and described briefly but vividly the reception it got.

Next day Gruenther returned to Vienna and called on Zheltov. The Russian General met us at the door of his office and shook hands cordially with Gruenther. When I put out my hand, Zheltov ostentatiously put his behind his back. We sat at the table.

"Anything wrong between you two?" Gruenther started breezily.

"Thayer insulted me yesterday," Zheltov began.

"What! Thayer insulted you? What did he say?" Gruenther acted as though he'd never heard of yesterday's explosion.

Zheltov repeated in Russian what I'd said. His interpreter translated.

"Why, that's exactly what Clark told him to tell you, Zheltov. You wouldn't hold it against him that he obeys orders, would you?"

Gruenther leaned over and slapped Zheltov on the back. "Come on, fellow, don't be so damn stuffy. You didn't like Clark's message. He didn't expect you to. But you wouldn't take it out on a poor subordinate officer."

Zheltov at first glared but gradually, under Gruenther's grinning affability, he melted. Solemnly he rose, came around the table behind me and stuck out his hand.

"I'm sorry I didn't shake hands when you came in," he said in a low voice. We shook and he went back to his seat.

Peace reestablished, we settled down to business to discover not entirely to our surprise that the Russians were now prepared to accept most of our terms.

A few days after our meeting with Zheltov, the Allied Council met for the first time in Vienna. Tolbukhin had meanwhile been replaced by short bullet-headed, Marshal Koniev, who'd commanded the First Ukrainian Front. Koniev was a sociable sort of fellow and what he lacked in cunning and shrewdness was amply made up for by our friend General Zheltov who, to my regret, had not left with Tolbukhin.

The first meeting of the Council was held in the Grand Hotel, Soviet Headquarters in Vienna. The big issue was whether the Western Allies were prepared to recognize the

Austrian Government the Russians had set up with the old Austrian socialist, Karl Renner, as Chancellor.

Renner had been living more or less in exile in lower (eastern) Austria since Hitler had taken over in 1938. When the Russians captured the village where he was staying, Renner rejoiced briefly and remained quietly in his cottage. Little by little, rumors of the behavior of the Russian troops began to penetrate his seclusion. Tales of rape and looting and drunkenness became more and more alarming until the old man decided he'd better take a hand. So he put on his best Sunday-go-to-meeting suit and his top hat and marched down to the Russian Commandant's office where he proceeded to give the unfortunate Russian such unshirted hell that the man was speechless.

"You've come here as liberators," Renner told him, "and we welcomed you as such. But if your troops continue to behave like Mongolian hordes, you'll find that the Austrians and above all, the Viennese, are not apt to accept you as friends but as enemies and beasts. If on the other hand you behave like true socialists, Socialist Vienna will accept you with open arms."

The Commandant inquired by whom he was having the honor of being bawled out and Renner told him, "By one of Austria's oldest socialists." The Russian was so impressed that he sent a radio to Zheltov. Zheltov (who told us this story) sent for Renner who repeated his warning in even more explicit terms. Zheltov cabled Moscow. Moscow was even more impressed and told Zheltov to offer Renner the job of forming a government as soon as Vienna was liberated. Renner was no Communist but as a socialist he had no violent quarrel with communism as a Marxian theory. As a practical form of politics, however, Renner soon enough found out what Stalin's communism was like and reacted appropriately.

So when the Russians asked us to recognize the Government of the Socialist, Renner, we paused to consider. We would like to see what the rest of Austria in the British, French and American zones thought of the Government, we said, before we imposed this particular set of ministers on the whole country. We were prepared, said Clark, to recognize *a* government of Austria but not *the* Government of Austria until we thought it over.

"But it is a very nice government," Koniev argued soothingly. "It only has a few Communists in it." We'd agreed, he said, that Austria was a liberated country and needed a government. Why not recognize the Government and get along with the job?

Clark got stubborn. Koniev got stubborn.

"God damn it, Koniev, this is no way to play ball. We'll never get to first base at this rate."

Baseball was about as incomprehensible to Koniev as *Pravda* would have been to Clark. The Russian interpreter saw my dilemma and smiled. With a wink to him I switched metaphors to a more internationally known sport.

"General Clark says this is no way to play soccer. At this rate no one is going to score."

"Then I suggest the General start by giving the ball a good swift kick," Koniev replied, and the interpreter translated literally.

"Kick the ball? What kind of player do you take me for?" Clark said angrily, thinking Koniev was casting aspersions on his sportsmanship.

I thought it time to intervene before the situation got completely out of hand.

"You see, General, if you use baseball terms, the Russians won't exactly understand. . . ."

But Clark never enjoyed taking advice from junior officers.

"You just stick to translating and never mind telling me what to do," he interrupted. "Now tell Koniev we want to recognize *a* government for Austria, but not necessarily *the* Government of Austria. And be damn sure you get that straight." He glared at me as I translated.

"Now just to be sure, what's the word for 'a' in Russian?" Clark asked.

"There isn't any," I replied.

Clark's jaw muscles began to ripple.

"All right, God damn it, have it your way. Then what's the Russian word for 'the'?"

"There isn't any," I answered.

Clark exploded at General Gruenther, "What the hell kind of an interpreter is this man? Can't you get me someone who at least knows the words?"

At that point I was beginning to get a trifle sore myself.

But Koniev's Russian interpreter broke in.

"General, Thayer is quite right," he said firmly and emphatically. "There is no word for '*a*' or '*the*' in Russian but he has translated your meaning entirely accurately."

Clark subsided, and the Acting French Commander, General Cherriere, always a good friend in need, quickly raised another point on the agenda.

A few days later, the troops of the Western Allies arrived in Vienna. Naturally a review was in order. There was a little wrangling about which troops marched first, but that was soon settled. There was a good deal of staff work necessary to combine four different ways of having a review but that also was settled more or less satisfactorily.

As the four Commanders in their most gaudy uniforms marched front and center, their four interpreters followed solemnly behind, not quite so resplendent. Then we proceeded to the reviewing stand and took our places behind our respective bosses.

The American contingent marched past, snappily rigged out in green silk kerchiefs, white helmets and gloves. The British marched past in battle-jackets and berets. The Russians goose-stepped by the stand, their rifles with bayonets fixed, held horizontally before them as though to make sure the fellow in front wouldn't stop. Finally the French colonial troops marched past headed by a gorgeously dressed band complete with the traditional goat.

From time to time the Commanders exchanged compliments and we interpreters went into action.

"Your troops look mighty fit, General."

"So do yours, Marshal."

"Those are fine soldiers you have, Marshal."

"Yours are a fine lot, too, General."

My back began to ache from standing so long but eventually the ordeal ended.

After the parade, a newspaperman who'd been watching the ceremony from beside the stand asked me what all the talk on the reviewing stand had been about. Apparently he suspected the Commanders were using the opportunity to settle some weighty problems.

"To tell you the truth," I answered, "the only spontaneous remark I heard the whole time was when the French band came by and Marshal Koniev shouted gleefully, 'Oh, General, look at that goat!'"

For a month or so after the review, relations between the Western Allies and the Russians were cordial enough, though from time to time there'd be a slight spat—usually when the Russians thought they were being left out or snubbed. It was the custom when the Allied Council met for the Acting Chairman to give a lunch in the noon-break and, if the meeting went on long enough, a tea or cocktails afterwards.

The first time Clark was Chairman, his mess sergeant had run out of matches to put by the ashtrays. Knowing that the OSS mess was usually the best provided in town, he went to my mess sergeant and borrowed several boxes of paper matches of which we had an enormous supply. The only difficulty was that they were left-overs from an operation some OSS screwball had dreamed up for use just before the Normandy landings, which consisted of dropping match boxes instead of pamphlets on our French Allies. On the outside cover were the flags of France, England and the United States. On the inside cover were some terse instructions about how to blow up a bridge. Whether they ever actually dropped any of the matches I don't know. But I do know that when the war was over we were shipped case after case for our own use.

As we sat down to lunch that day, General Zheltov's eyes lit on the matches with the three flags on the covers. He passed a box to Koniev with a muttered comment. Koniev turned to Clark.

"May I ask, General," he said acidly, "why you have seen fit to leave the Russian flag off your matches?"

Clark stared at the matches, gulped and called for the mess sergeant.

"Where the hell did these matches come from?"

"Oh, Colonel Thayer's outfit loaned them to me," said the sergeant innocently.

A withering glare caught my eye across the table.

"We'll let Thayer explain that one, Marshal," Clark snarled.

I told Koniev what the matches had been made for and he seemed slightly mollified.

As we left the table Clark whispered to his mess sergeant to get some other matches before the next recess.

When we sat down to tea some hours later Koniev immediately reached for a box of matches. This time there

were no flags, but some writing on them. He showed them to
Clark.

"What does that say?"

Clark gulped again and told me to translate.

With more than a little relish, I translated the inscrip-
tion.

"It says, 'You don't *have* to have venereal disease,' Marshal."

There was a prolonged silence until it was time to go back
to work.

Marshal Koniev was a very likable old fellow, and I think
inherently decent. When, on instructions from Moscow, he
had to get down on his front paws and growl like a bear, he
did it reluctantly and not very convincingly. He didn't seem
very shrewd and I've no way of judging what sort of a military strategist he was. But then I was always a little bearish
about the brilliance of Soviet strategy.

Once a well-known American military commentator came
to Vienna along with several high-ranking dignitaries. General Clark gave a cocktail party for them to which Koniev
came without his interpreter. So I stuck close to him and
translated what had to be translated.

The American military commentator was particularly anxious to discuss strategy with Koniev. He started out effu-
sively:

"Marshal, I just want to tell you how much I admired
your particular military strategy during the war."

The Marshal looked taken aback.

"Yes, I followed your First Ukrainian Front with especial
interest because, so it seemed to me at least, you showed a
real genius for taking advantage of the basic military factors
as they presented themselves."

Koniev looked puzzled.

"Yes, Marshal, as you advanced across Eastern Europe, I made a very careful study of every move you made. They were so carefully thought out, so beautifully timed and so precisely executed I really think they rank among the masterpieces of military history."

Koniev began to look weary but the commentator went bubbling on.

"Yes, Marshal, and the best was when you reached Germany and were approaching Dresden. I remember when you got to the confluence of the Elbe and the Polzen rivers, I asked myself: now what is Koniev going to do? Will he go north to strike at the German center or will he turn south and outflank the panzers? And you remember what you did. You went west. It was positively brilliant!"

Koniev was looking bored to death. But the commentator kept at it:

"And then when you reached the head of the valley near Dresden, again I said to myself, 'He's done it again. He's captured the initiative. [The Germans had been retreating for two years.] He's got the advantage of multiple alternatives.' That's what I said to myself, Marshal, and I tried to guess again what you'd do. North? South? I decided you'd strike south and I was wrong again. You struck west right into Dresden and captured it. That's real genius."

Koniev yawned.

"Come on," he muttered, catching me by the arm, "let's go and talk to General Gruenther." When he was out of earshot of the military commentator, he murmured:

"What the devil was that man talking about? North? South? Hell, doesn't he know Germany's *west* of Russia?"

Fitzroy MacLean used to say that Soviet military strategy could best be summed up in one command: "Put a little hay in your cart, soldier, and go west."

After Tolbukhin had departed with his slightly rougher-than-necessary troops of the Third Ukrainian Front, Zheltov, his deputy, had, as I said, remained on as Koniev's deputy. The relationship of a Soviet marshal to his immediate staff is different from that of an American general to his staff. According to Zheltov, the command of a Soviet Army Group is vested in three men, the Marshal, his Political Deputy (Zheltov) and the Chief of the Administrative Services. The last has a say in decisions only when administrative problems are up for discussion. The Political Deputy, according to Zheltov, has a say in all decisions but may be overruled in a pinch by the Marshal. He does have the right, however, of communicating directly with the Central Committee of the Communist Party in Moscow and the Party may support him and overrule the Marshal. In that case the Marshal had better change his mind or start packing. Zheltov said that he'd been with Tolbukhin most of the war and only twice had he disagreed with him. In both cases the Marshal had been proved right (i.e., the Kremlin had turned down Zheltov's objectives).

I often tried to find out what the position of the GPU troops was in the chain of command. (Strictly speaking the Soviet Secret Police were no longer called GPU but NKVD and later MVD.) Were they responsible to the Field Commander or directly to Moscow? GPU troops generally lagged behind the fighting troops. It was almost ten days after the fighting troops had moved through Belgrade that the Soviet Secret Police began to make themselves conspicuous. Once Germany had capitulated, security functions in the occupied (or liberated) zones seem to have been monopolized by the GPU who appeared to enjoy complete autonomy from the Field Commander. I found this out by bitter experience.

Once we'd moved to Vienna, in the heart of the Soviet

Zone, I had to give up my weekend hunting trips, since it was ordinarily impossible to hunt in the Soviet Zone and it took too long to get to the American Zone and back. One day, between interpreting bouts, I asked Koniev if he wouldn't give me a pass to hunt in the Soviet Zone. He quickly agreed and the next day sent me a so-called grey pass, signed personally by himself, permitting me to go wherever I wanted in the Soviet Zone.

A young Viennese aristocrat whom we shall call "Nicky," whose family had had a large estate two hours south of Vienna, had invited me to shoot a stag in his family's forests. So with Koniev's pass we set off one Saturday in a jeep.

When we arrived in the village where the family estate was, we found that the castle had been taken over by Soviet troops. So we went to the village priest's house and he put us up.

I hadn't been asleep long when there was a knock on the bedroom door and a young Soviet soldier walked in.

Would the American officer, he asked, please get dressed and come down to the village military police headquarters?

I protested that I was getting up early next morning to shoot, that I needed the sleep and that I had a pass signed by Marshal Koniev giving me permission to be there. Couldn't they wait until after the shoot?

But the soldier said he had his orders and that was that.

Annoyed, I dressed and went to the village police post. As I walked in, six or eight soldiers were lolling about the room sleeping or playing cards. At a desk sat a young GPU lieutenant, red cap on head, a cigarette hanging from his lips. He looked up as I stood in the doorway and casually motioned me to his desk. I was tempted to call him to attention but figured he would only get sore and possibly spoil my shooting.

So I came in and sat down.

"What are you doing here?" the Lieutenant asked.

"Hunting," I said.

"Who are you?"

I tossed him the pass Koniev had given me written in Russian.

He read it but seemed singularly unimpressed.

"What's your real reason for coming here?"

I began to get sore but decided it was best to be sweetly reasonable.

"I've told you my reason, Lieutenant."

The Lieutenant abruptly changed his tack.

"Why has the United States abandoned its friendly policy to Russia since the war ended?"

It seemed a slightly odd question for a young Soviet officer to be asking me in the middle of the night in a small Austrian village. But he was evidently getting down to what he thought were brass tacks. The soldiers lying about dozing and playing cards suddenly sat up and began to take an interest. What would the American say to that?

"Don't be an ass," I answered. "There's been absolutely no change in the American attitude to Russia, but there may well be if you treat us with the uncultured insolence you're showing me."

At the word "uncultured" the Lieutenant winced but then recovered himself.

"We must be vigilant," he protested. He picked up a Red Army newspaper from his desk. "Read what it says here," and he pointed to a long editorial on the front page. "See what you Americans are up to."

I glanced through the article hurriedly. I can't remember exactly what it was about but it insinuated pretty clearly that we and the British were trying to undermine the Czechoslovak People's Government they were setting up in Prague.

"That's a lot of nonsense," I said tossing down the paper.

There was a long silence.

"Well, Lieutenant, I guess you've found out what you wanted to know. I'm off to bed as I have to get up at five to go shooting."

The Lieutenant looked a little worried. His shot in the dark had obviously missed the target.

"Well, I'll have to telephone to Division Headquarters and tell them you're here. I'm sure everything will be all right." He wasn't sure at all. Nor was I.

"And just one more thing. Someone told us the fellow with you is a prince. Is that right?"

"Yes," I said, "he's a prince."

"A real, full-ranking prince?" the Lieutenant asked.

"All prince and a yard wide," I assured him.

"Do you think it would be all right if we asked him to stop in and have a glass of tea?"

"You can invite him over," I said, "but you mustn't order him."

"Can we say you're having tea with us?"

I said they could.

There was a bustle of activity as one of the soldiers dashed off after some hot water. A tea pot, already half full of a thick brew of soaking tea leaves, was put on the table. Glasses, spoons and even some sugar appeared.

A few minutes later a terrified Austrian prince was standing in the doorway. He gave one look at me as though I'd risen from the dead.

"Are you all right?" he murmured apprehensively.

"Sure! Come on in. They just wanted to see what an Austrian prince looks like."

Nicky looked a little mollified but not exactly gay.

The Austrian Prince was given the place of honor. The Colonel from America, Russia's great ally, was left to shift for himself.

Nicky was vastly relieved when we finally said goodnight and went to bed.

At five the next morning we were up and ready to start. I got into the jeep and someone went to open the yard gate onto the street. Outside stood a large Soviet soldier complete with tommygun. My heart sank but I put the car in gear and started out. The soldier raised his gun. I shouted for him to get out of the way.

"You're not going anywhere," he retorted insolently. "Them's my orders."

I insisted he send for his commanding officer and swore and threatened him for ten minutes. But I might as well have been talking to the apple tree in the garden. I stormed around the village looking for the Lieutenant but he was keeping well out of sight.

An hour passed before another lieutenant and a soldier appeared.

"We're very sorry but they telephoned from Division Headquarters during the night to say they'd like to have a little chat with you before you go shooting. It won't keep you long."

In spite of all my protests they insisted and a half hour later we drove up to Division Headquarters in the next town. I was ushered into an office occupied by a GPU major and several subordinates. The major greeted me politely, even gingerly.

He took a piece of paper and pencil and began a series of questions:

"Name? Place of birth? Rank? Nationality?"

I tried to keep my patience.

"Here is my pass, issued and signed personally by Marshal Koniev. He knows all about me and he gave orders that I be permitted to go shooting here. Are you or are you not under Koniev's command?"

The Major blinked and thought a moment.

"In a manner of speaking we are, of course, under Koniev's orders." It was equivalent to saying, "Hell, no, we're not under Koniev and that pass means nothing to us."

He wrote down the data from the pass and then sat back.

"Of course, you know how many divisions we have in this area, don't you, Colonel?"

At first I didn't get what he was driving at. "No, I don't have the vaguest idea—and what's that got to do with my going stag shooting?"

"Well, you know the designation of the local division, of course, and now you've even learned where our headquarters are. Have you been able to make any estimate of our troop strength?"

Then it dawned on me.

"Look here, Major," I said, "if you're accusing me of spying on your God-damned troops, please be very careful. I don't know and I don't give a damn what troops you have here. All I've discovered is that you've got more than the average quota of intolerably stupid, insolent officers. And you can be sure I'll report that to General Clark and to Washington."

The Major could see I wasn't putting on any act. I was mad. He figured he'd made a mistake and started to back track.

"I'm sorry we've inconvenienced you, but you know we have to be careful about strangers, foreigners, in this area. But we won't detain you any longer. You can go now and shoot all the stags you want."

I looked at my watch. It was already ten-thirty. "This is a fine time to tell me. If you knew anything about it you'd realize it's far too late to go hunting now. I'm going back to Vienna right now and tell Koniev what happened."

Nicky and I climbed back into the jeep and headed for

home. We were about half way to Vienna, passing through
the main square of a small town when I stopped to ask the
way from a Russian soldier armed with a rifle and bayonet.
I realized almost at once it was a stupid thing to do but by
that time the soldier had his bayonet pointed at my stomach
and was ordering me out of the car. I protested as usual. A
crowd of Austrians gathered to watch the Russian holding
up an American officer. For the third time in twenty-four
hours I'd been arrested by the Russians. I bounded out of the
jeep and told the soldier to take me to his commanding
officer. Since that was obviously what he was going to do
anyway, I thought I'd better put the best possible face on it
in front of our Austrian spectators.

I was taken to the Town Hall and allowed to sit for half
an hour waiting for the Town Commandant. When he finally turned up in the usual MVD uniform, I went right
into the attack. I told him who I was, why I had gone into the
Zone, what had happened to me the night before, what had
happened at Division Headquarters, and now what had happened right outside his window. Until the soldier apologized
publicly, I added, I was going to stay in his office.

The unfortunate Commandant, also a major, was somewhat taken aback at this outburst.

"But, Colonel, I'm most awfully sorry. I promise no insult
was intended. I'll certainly have the soldier apologize to you,
but not publicly. After all we're in occupation here and we
must safeguard our prestige among the townspeople."

"In the town square," I repeated and, folding my arms, sat
back in my chair.

The Major pleaded but I didn't even answer. A half hour
went by.

"Colonel, let's compromise. I'll have the soldier apologize
in front of my staff here in the assembly hall."

As I was beginning to get hungry I accepted.

Ten minutes later fifteen or twenty officers were rounded up from the mess hall and the unfortunate soldier, minus his rifle, his round cap twisting nervously in his hand, appeared in the doorway. He looked as though he were about to burst into tears.

"I'm sorry," he murmured, "that I stuck my bayonet in your stomach."

The soldier and the officers filed out, leaving me alone with the Major.

"Now there's just one more thing, Major, I must ask of you."

The Major looked discouraged. When was he ever going to get rid of this importunate American?

"I want you to assign one of your GPU soldiers to act as my escort back to Vienna. I've been arrested enough today."

The Major looked relieved. He could arrange that easily.

A few minutes later I walked out into the town square to find my friend Nicky perspiring with heat and worry in the jeep.

"What's this fellow?" he asked suspiciously pointing to the red-capped GPU soldier following me.

"That's our escort," I answered proudly. "He's going to try to keep us from getting arrested any more today."

As we drove into Vienna I asked our young GPU man whether he wanted to be dropped at Marshal Koniev's headquarters at the Grand Hotel.

"If you don't mind, I'd rather you dropped me at our headquarters," he replied.

" 'Our' headquarters? Where's that?"

"You know, the Secret Police building over near the river."

I had the answer to the question of what control a Russian field commander had over the political police. But it was certainly the hard way to find out.

Korea, yesterday, today and tomorrow

after the first orgy of international friendship when the G.I.'s and the Russkis met at the Oder, they each stood back and took a cooler look at the other and weren't particularly pleased. The G.I.'s chewing gum, cigarettes and snappy uniforms seemed to give the Russkis a certain inferiority complex which they hid behind a noisy swagger not designed to inspire any great love or affection from the G.I.'s. But after a while they got used to each other and settled down to an uneasy unarmed truce which has somehow managed to last to this day in Vienna. Every now and then one of them would take a pot shot at the other or lob a bottle across a barroom or even steal the affections of an Austrian fraulein. But the quadripartite police jeeps organized by the Russian and Allied Provost Marshals somehow managed to untangle brawlers without too much loss of blood and face.

Clark and Koniev, Gruenther and Zheltov, too, became accustomed to each other's idiosyncrasies and managed to develop a tolerable working arrangement. Clark got himself an interpreter who knew all the Russian words, though I sometimes wondered superciliously whether he knew what they meant. Gruenther got an intensive course in understanding the Russians from Zheltov and before long there wasn't much for me to do. Even the OSS professors made it clear they could get along without my amateur help.

One day I got a message from the State Department reminding me that I'd been loaned to OSS for the Yugoslav job which was now over. How about coming back to the Foreign Service and taking an assignment in the Embassy at Moscow? I answered that I was always available for any assignment but that I was still under obligations to General Donovan and besides I'd already done two tours in Moscow. I would almost rather go back there, I added, than shoot myself. Nevertheless, I told them sententiously, I was always ready to do my duty.

I didn't hear from the Department again for some time. Then the OSS suggested I take on a job in Germany. I explained apologetically that I was only on loan from the State Department and hesitated to take on another mission now that the war was over. The OSS subsided for a while.

A week or two later the War Department hinted at a transfer from Vienna but I told them of my commitments to the State Department and OSS. They eventually dropped the idea, too, and I went about my leisurely way cultivating the Viennese art of drinking coffee, talking a lot and doing nothing.

Then OSS in Washington suggested that I try to find out how the Russians were doing in their newly acquired

Danubian colonies. So I took off on a tour of the Balkans.
My first stop was Budapest. It was a sad, dreary rubble heap
of its former self. An American diplomatic and military
mission were already supplying Washington with the de-
pressing details of the Soviet occupation. So as soon as I could
I came back to Vienna.

Then I got a plane from ATC and set out for Bucharest.
En route we landed at my old hunting grounds at Zemun
to refuel. That is, all but one wheel landed. It remained hidden in its hideaway in the fuselage. The plane skidded, and
lurched, spun around and finally came to a stop leaning
drunkenly on one rumpled wing. I wired Vienna for a re-
placement for my plane and sat down to wait. Belgrade had
changed little in six months except that the Government was
growing up and growing more self-conscious.

After I'd checked in at the Embassy, I called on my old
friend, General Kisiliev, the head of the Soviet Military Mission. He seemed delighted to see me and though it was only
about ten in the morning he cracked open a liter of vodka
and a kilo or so of caviar. For an hour or more we rem-
inisced and bewailed the passing of the good old days
when there were no embassies—just military missions. Kisiliev asked me what plans I had and I told him of my intention of visiting Bucharest and the crack-up on Zemun.

"You want to go to Bucharest? Take my plane." He rang
a bell and an aide appeared. "Have my plane set up for
Bucharest tomorrow. What time do you want to leave?" he
asked.

"Around noon would be fine."

"Tell the plane to be ready at 3:30 p.m. and tell the cook
Colonel Thayer is having lunch with me tomorrow."

Next day, after a somewhat liquid lunch, I was whisked
down to the airfield in a Soviet limousine, climbed aboard a
battered old Soviet *"Duglas,"* as they called their C-47's, and

was on my way to Bucharest. The ceiling at Bucharest couldn't have been more than a foot off the ground when we landed but somehow or other the pilot hit the runway square and I got down from the plane shaking and sweating but otherwise undamaged.

General Schuyler, the head of our Military Mission in Bucharest, seemed a bit startled to see me, as no American planes had been allowed to land at Bucharest for a week on account of the weather. I told him I'd come in a plane the Russians had lent me. He seemed even more startled. "The Russians lent an American a plane to fly around the Balkans! It's unheard of!" I told him about Kisiliev and how for almost a year he'd been not only a good friend but a very cooperative and helpful colleague.

Schuyler shook his head. "Well, there's no denying there must be Russians and Russians. The only trouble is the Russians who set the pace aren't the Kisiliev's." From there we launched into a long discussion of why the Kremlin seemed so determined to make enemies of us. As usual, we found no answer.

Bucharest for the first three or four days was superb. Everywhere you turned there were caviar, foie gras and gypsy music. For four days I lived on a diet of all three. I spent the next few days in bed. A local doctor said it was just my digestion and I didn't see any reason to disagree with him.

About that time the Council of Foreign Ministers was meeting in Moscow and the question arose whether the Soviets were living up to their promise made at Yalta to allow the liberated countries to choose their own governments according to democratic rules. Specifically we questioned whether a recent visit of Vyshinski to Bucharest, during which he'd ordered King Michael to fire his Prime Minister, had anything in common with democracy. As a result of the dispute they agreed to send Vyshinski and Ambassadors Harriman and Clark-Kerr down to Bucharest to see if they couldn't "broaden the base of the Government." It was a rather futile trip as Harriman was well aware but at least we had to try, even if it meant running the risk, as one irreverent observer put it, of getting our own bases broadened in the process.

I was sitting in the lobby of the Athenee Plaza Hotel recovering from my overdose of caviar, foie gras and gypsies when Harriman arrived.

"We've just been talking about you in Moscow," he told me. "I'd like to have a little chat with you." Despite his smile it sounded ominous.

Upstairs in his room, Harriman produced a bottle of Scotch, poured two good drinks and began chatting about the results of the Conference. He said they'd discussed the German and Austrian problems and reparations and several other hot issues.

"We also came to an agreement about Korea."

He paused and gave me a sidelong glance.

"We decided to set up a joint Commission to unite north and south Korea."

He paused again, waiting for a reaction from me. But I scarcely knew where Korea was and innocently sipped the excellent Scotch.

"It's a very important place, Korea," Harriman continued, "and the negotiations are going to be very difficult. We'll have to have someone there who knows something about the way the Soviets operate. Very important job indeed." He paused again. A faint glimmering of light began to dawn. Harriman went on:

"It's an interesting place they tell me, Seoul. Not Paris or London exactly, but interesting—very interesting. And the Koreans, I'm told, are very interesting, too. First chance they'll have had to run their government since 1906 or something like."

"It sounds pretty awful to me," I commented.

"Oh, it won't be too bad," Harriman answered with a sinister smile. "One might even enjoy it. Now let's go down and get some dinner."

He got up and the conversation ended in mid-air.

It was obvious enough what Harriman was trying to tell me, but I reassured myself that for six months I'd been successfully playing off State, War and OSS whenever someone cooked up a new assignment for me. I was confident—over-confident—that I could do it again.

For three weeks I was weatherbound in Bucharest. No planes either came in from the west or departed in that direction. All the Danube bridges were blown up and the river had just enough ice to stop the ferries and not enough to hold a jeep. So I sat and fattened on caviar and foie gras and exercised to the tune of gypsy music in Bucharest's nightclubs with Harriman's charming and peripatetic daughter, Kathleen.

At last a plane came in and I returned to Vienna where a telegram was waiting for me.

"You are assigned to the Joint U.S.-U.S.S.R. Commission for Korea. Proceed to Seoul at once via Washington. The State and War Departments concur," it ended peremptorily. With all three of my bosses in rare agreement my goose was cooked.

In Washington they told me as much as they knew about Korea, which didn't take very long.

"But how am I supposed to play it?" I asked hoping for some sort of instructions.

"By ear," they replied as usual. Then they sent me on my way.

At Tokyo airport I ran into Averell and Kathleen Harriman who were on their way home from Moscow flying east.

"We've just been in Seoul," Harriman said, "and it's just as I thought: very, very interesting." He grinned his most sinister grin.

Harriman was right as far as he went. Seoul was interesting. When I reported in Seoul to the Commanding General, John Hodge, he took one look at my silver leaves and snorted:

"What! Just a lieutenant colonel! Hell, I thought they were sending me some rank. The political man on the Soviet side has the rank of a lieutenant general."

I apologized and explained that I had nothing to do with the War Department's promotion system. Besides, I explained, in my last few assignments I'd always maintained that I ranked with, but after, marshals. Hodge grunted and hunched his shoulders with three stars on them.

"Who do you work for?" Hodge asked.

"Well, that's a bit complicated. As near as I can figure it out, State loaned me to War in 1944. War loaned me to OSS. OSS loaned me back to War in 1945 and if I'm not mistaken War has now loaned me back to State."

"Well, the first thing to do is to take those damn silver leaves off."

I was faintly proud of and much attached to my leaves. "When must I get rid of them?"

"Right now," and Hodge seized them in both hands and snatched them off. I rather hoped he'd prick his fingers but he didn't.

"Now if anyone asks you, tell 'em you have the assimilated rank of a general. Don't specify what kind of a general and don't say lieutenant general either." He shrugged his three star shoulders again.

"And you'll stay at the VIP Chosen Hotel," he added.

That news cheered me up till I saw the Chosen Hotel. In Vienna we wouldn't have used it for a transient recruits' billet. The thought of Vienna put a lump in my throat. There I'd had a whole hotel, the Golden Stag, to myself and my staff with a Viennese chef and Viennese cooking and Viennese wine. The Chosen had an army cook. I'm sure he was clean. Everything was boiled till the last microbe and all the taste had died. Instead of venison and trout and caviar, we had standard army rations, except when General Mac-Arthur's supply sergeants pirated our shipments as they passed through Japan. Then we lived on an emergency ration of frankfurters and sauerkraut three times a day.

"I'll have a room with bath," I told the clerk.

"There are no rooms with baths," he answered.

"Then I guess I'll just have a room. What time is the diningroom open for breakfast?"

"Six-thirty to seven."

"In the morning?" I asked incredulously.

"In the morning," the expressionless oriental repeated. "General Hodge's orders," he explained.

"Then be good enough to send me up a tray at eight-thirty. I'll eat in my room. Just a boiled egg, a little fruit and coffee."

"No room service. No fruit—canned juice. No eggs—just powder," the clerk informed me.

"Good God, man. Do you suppose General Hodge has heard that the war's over?"

The clerk's face was as impassive as ever. "He knows."

I went up to a diminutive room and compared it sadly with my comfortable suite in the Golden Stag. I tried the water in the washbasin. It didn't run, hot or cold.

"We'll fill the tank upstairs right away," the porter promised.

I flopped down on the bed.

"What the hell's interesting about this?" I thought.

I was still thinking when I felt a drop of water on my face.

The ceiling was soaked and soon water was pouring all over the place. I shouted down the hall for the porter. He examined the ceiling.

"Water-tank overflowed," he explained with that wooden oriental expression.

For the six months I was there, it was always the same. Either there was no water at all or it ran both from the tap and the ceiling.

The morning after I arrived in Seoul I sauntered into the General's office around nine o'clock, breakfastless.

"The General's staff meeting is at seven-thirty every morning, Mr. Thayer," his adjutant said rather pointedly.

I acted as if I hadn't heard a word.

"General in?" I asked.

He was. For a few minutes Hodge discussed the problem confronting us with the Russians who, as yet, hadn't appeared for the negotiations. Then he sent me to see General Archie Arnold who was to head the American side of the Commission.

General Arnold was like General Hodge, a general's general but, also like Hodge, he had far more than an average share of common sense, native shrewdness and humor. With those three attributes you should be able to "handle the Russians" with one hand behind your back, I thought. And Arnold did.

With him Arnold had several very competent colonels and a fabulous Lieutenant Bertsch who not only had learned the incredibly difficult language but had made himself the confidant of almost every politician in Korea.

Several weeks elapsed before the Russians turned up to negotiate the reunification of Korea. In the meantime, we prepared our briefs and worked with the South Korean politicians toward a satisfactory position for the negotiations.

On the seventeen thousand mile journey from Vienna to

Seoul I'd read all the histories of Korea I could lay hands on. For several days I questioned General Arnold and his staff about the current situation. By then it was clear that Hodge and Arnold had just about every card in the pack against them.

Centuries ago Korea had been an independent state. Then she had become a semi-vassal of the Chinese Empire to which she paid tribute. Under many of her rulers Korean civilization had flourished. She boasted the oldest phonetic alphabet in the world. As the Chinese Empire fell apart in the nineteenth century, Korea, than a monarchy, had regained a precarious independence threatened from the north by the Russians and from the east by Japan. During a series of palace revolutions, Korea oscillated between Russian and Japanese hegemony. Finally as a result of the Russo-Japanese war Japan established a protectorate over the Kingdom and early in the twentieth century formally annexed the country and established a colonial government. All Korean political life was forbidden and Koreans were replaced by Japanese in just about every post higher than elevator boy. Thus for almost forty years the Koreans had been deprived of every sort of political life except for a handful of fanatical patriots who went into exile in Shanghai, Chungking and Washington where they devoted themselves to keeping alive the spark of Korean independence.

In the Autumn of 1945, when Hodge arrived, every last man, woman and child of the Japanese Colonial Administration was packed off home. Except for the handful of exiles like Syngman Rhee, Kim Koo and half a dozen others who began to trickle home, there was scarcely a Korean with any political or administrative experience among the thirty odd million inhabitants of the penninsula to take the place of the departing Japanese. With a few hundred American Civil Affairs officers, Hodge had to set up a central administration

as well as a system of regional governments. How he did it is
a miracle I shall never understand. With great foresight he
required that for every American administrator there should
be a Korean understudy who eventually would take over the
job. This took care of the formal administration but the building of genuine political parties was something only the
Koreans could do on their own initiative.

On top of that, there was the 38th Parallel, originally set
up as a boundary line for Allied and Russian warships in the
Japanese and Yellow Seas. When it came to occupying the
country, MacArthur's staff found they could spare neither
the men nor the ships to occupy the whole country. Further-
more, the Red Army began pouring down from the north as
soon as Hirohito capitulated. So a hasty agreement was made
with the Russians, extending the existing water boundary
across the island as a zonal dividing line. Politically, economi-
cally or geographically it made little sense except that it
divided the country roughly in half but in so doing it followed no existing provincial, or geographic boundaries. It
split the twelve million Northern Koreans from the eighteen
million Southern Koreans. It separated the basic extracting
industries of the north from the manufacturing industries of
the south. It even cut the main power lines that fed Seoul
from the hydroelectric plants of the Yalu River.

Thus ancient traditions, Japanese enslavement, Allied liberation and finally partition all combined to produce a rare
degree of political pandemonium by 1946. There was no
political authority outside the occupation forces, few experi-
enced political leaders, no political parties and very little
genuine political understanding among the leaders of what
Korea's real interests were. Into the resulting vacuum the
Communists spilled like water over Niagara. The Communist Party which had managed more or less to keep going underground during the Japanese government, surfaced in full

regalia almost before Hodge got ashore. But as usual, the Red Army hordes in the north soon acquired a reputation for rape, pillage and terror that drove the northerners down across the 38th Parallel in hundreds of thousands, each with his personal horror story.

Before the war we used to think the best treatment for would-be Communists was to come to Moscow and watch them operate for a while. "The Moscow cure," we called it. After the war we decided there was an even better cure: get liberated by the Red Army. No propaganda campaign in the world could compete with it. It was no less effective in Korea than it was in Eastern Europe.

Soon after our troops had landed, other political parties began to organize. Synghman Rhee, the most prominent and well-heeled of the returning exiles, promptly got his party into action. An energetic but inexperienced group started a liberal People's Party which attracted many who found Synghman Rhee too conservative and the Communists too tainted by the barbarities of the north. Whereupon, with considerable ingenuity, Communist operatives got to work and by bribery, threat and skillful maneuvering captured the People's National Committee and with it, the party.

The leaders of the People's Party, Lyuh Woon Hyung, had had an American education and had even learned to play baseball. Some of the political psychologists on General Hodge's staff thereupon jumped to the conclusion that Lyuh's knowledge of baseball would immunize him from the Communist virus. To their surprise and chagrin, they soon found out that you can't fight political battles with baseball bats— even American bats. Lyuh remained loyal to his Communist masters until he was assassinated a year later with a sawed-off shotgun. The Russians maintained it was an American shotgun but we indignantly denied the slander pointing out

that political murders were not part of the democratic process.

Soon a welter of smaller parties began to be formed wherever two or three people with political ambition, a typewriter and an automobile gathered together. There were
Marxian socialist parties, anti-Marxian socialist parties, socialist parties, patriotic parties, international parties, peasant
parties. In all, some thirty existed by the time I got there in
February 1946. But with the exception of Rhee's Party, the
Communists' stooge People's Party, and a couple of others,
none had much of a following.

Being a bit inexperienced in political matters some of the
minor leaders came to us for advice in drawing up their
platforms. My first job, a day or two after my arrival in Seoul,
was to help draft a platform for a leftist anti-Communist
group who wanted to win away the working class from the
Communists. After we'd included in the platform all the
traditional demands of workers' parties, it occurred to me we
might take a leaf or two from the Communists themselves so
we added a plank demanding "adequate social and medical
care for pregnant mothers." The Party was delighted with
this innovation and I considered we were making real progress against the Communists when a week or two later another leftist group published its platform with a plank demanding "adequate medical care for pregnant and lactating
mothers."

Rivalries between the various small parties soon became
intense, and strong-arm groups and private protection squads
began to be formed. Several politicians were shot, stabbed or
kidnapped before we could train a police force sufficiently
strong and non-political to maintain a degree of order.

The incompetents and the crooks were, however, a small
minority among the sincere public leaders who came forward.

There were a number of university graduates, some from American colleges, who immediately went to work to develop a genuinely democratic political system. Synghman Rhee for all his conservatism was a fanatical devotee of democratic government. Another was Kim Kiu Sik, a graduate, I think, of Princeton, who for a time was Prime Minister until his health gave out.

Unfortunately not all the best people were prepared to take a hand in the political development of the country. Sometimes I went with Lieutenant Bertsch as he travelled around the countryside visiting doctors, teachers, farmers and urging them to assume leadership in their communities. We would sit for hours cross-legged in the gardens of their country homes, sipping tea or rice wine and nibbling sweets, while we discussed the weather, the crops, the cost of living and at last our real objective, politics.

Back in Seoul almost every evening we would foregather with the leading politicians of all the "respectable," i.e., non-Communist, parties and talk over the coming negotiations with the Russians. The Moscow Conference directive under which we were to negotiate specified that in selecting a government for all Korea the Joint Commission should consult with all Korean democratic social and political organizations. Who were the reliable politicians, if any, in the north? What groups in the south could we rely on? Could the People's Party be freed from the tiny handful of Communist agents who had infiltrated it and seized control?

The Korean is by nature a rather excitable person. "Volatile" is the word historians usually use. "Fissionable" I sometimes thought would have been more accurate. Frequently these evening discussions got rather heated and on at least one occasion we had to pour water on one Cabinet Minister to bring his temperature back to normal. It must have been an appalling strain on our hosts to plan the future of their

own state with occidentals as ignorant as most of us were
of their ancient traditions, customs and exceedingly refined
mental processes. But somehow they put up with us and I
don't think our talks were entirely unproductive.

Up north across the 38th Parallel, different principles
were applied. Although several sincere and astute politicians
at first managed to organize genuinely democratic parties,
they soon found themselves in house arrest and their organizations disbanded. For example, the man the Russians had
originally picked to head the northern Council of Peoples
Soviets, a real democrat, Cho Man Sik, was put in house
arrest in January 1946 and has since disappeared completely.
In the place of the original parties, societies and associations
were set up under the leadership of elements "friendly to
the Soviet Union" for each social or economic interest. There
were unions for every branch of labor—all under a single
roof organization. Then there were associations of peasant
cooperatives, societies for cultural and professional workers,
a women's organization and, of course, a youth organization,
reminiscent of Mussolini's Giovanezza, or the Hitler Jugend,
or the Russians' Komsomols. All of these, completely domi-
nated by Soviet stooges, could be fully relied upon by our
Soviet colleagues in the forthcoming negotiations. We, on the
other hand, having permitted Communists and non-Communists to organize, couldn't trust at least two big parties in
the south and couldn't be entirely sure the Russians wouldn't
do a quick infiltration job on several other wobblers.

To add to our troubles, the Moscow Conferences had directed us to make recommendations to our Governments con-
cerning the possibility of putting the new Korean Government under some form of "trusteeship." Considering the
long period during which they'd been excluded from government, and the inevitable youth and weakness of their institu-
tions, the Foreign Ministers thought it not unreasonable

that some form of interim tutelage would be necessary until the Koreans could get back into the swing of running their own affairs. The Koreans, however, thought differently. Proud, self-confident and exceedingly sensitive to any implications that they couldn't govern themselves, those Koreans who were free to express themselves roundly denounced trusteeship and all its works. They had been a nation, they pointed out, while the Americans and Russians were still uncouth mobs of wild Indians and nomads.

While we waited for the Russians to come to Seoul to negotiate, we tried to explain to the southern Koreans the possible advantages of "trusteeship" which at least implied a form of protection against outside aggression. But the southern Koreans said they were quite competent to protect themselves. "Trasteeship," as they called it, stank and nothing we could say would change its smell.

At first we heard rumblings from Northern Korea along the same lines but then the "People's Democracy" of the Kremlin gradually went into action and one by one the "democratic and social organizations" of Northern Korea either shouted wildly for trusteeship or mysteriously went out of existence. It was impossible, the Russians explained, to be against something a democratic Soviet Foreign Minister wanted, and still be democratic. Hence to denounce trusteeship was undemocratic, hence fascist reactionary and against "the will of the people."

It was a convenient formula to eliminate from public life in Northern Korea anyone who didn't accept the Stalinist gospel. But it put them on the spot when it came to telling the Southern Korean Communists what to do. South of the 38th Parallel "trasteeship" had become anathema, though not one in a dozen knew what it meant. If the Southern Communists were to say "Hurrah for trusteeship," their goose as a political party was cooked.

Shortly after the Moscow decision became public, the South Koreans staged an enormous protest demonstration against "trasteeship." All the political parties were to take part. Frantically the Communists in Seoul appealed to their bosses in the north for instructions. Were they to refuse to take part and thus commit political harikiri or were they to join in the fun and denounce trusteeship, too? In Pyongyang, the "capital" of Northern Korea, the Communists scratched their heads and sucked the ends of their paint brushes: what instructions to write to their southern confederates? Apparently it was too much for them and they wired frantically to Big Brother in Moscow.

Meanwhile preparations had been completed for the demonstration in Seoul. All the parties were ready to fill the streets on the day set. Banners and placards had been prepared and covered with disparaging remarks about "trusteeship." The rank and file had been forewarned and were awaiting the call to turn out and shout against Russo-American imperialism. Everyone was ready except the Communists. They had cut out their placards and tacked up their banners and summoned their followers to be on tap. But as yet they didn't know what to write on the banners and placards or what to tell the faithful to shout.

The night before the parade there was anguish and turmoil in Communist headquarters in Seoul. The sign painters stood ready by the blank placards, paint and brush in hand. The Executive Committee locked itself in the secret council chamber and waited for the sentence to be pronounced from Pyongyang. Were they to commit suicide or not? And while they waited they apparently did something no good Bolshevik should ever do—they tried to think it all out for themselves. And the conclusion they reached was clear: independence is bad but suicide is worse.

Dawn broke. The time for the parade had arrived. Still

no word from Pyongyang. The strain became unbearable. Finally the doors of the Executive Committee room opened and the word went out:

"Down with Trusteeship!"

The painters set to work and before the placards were dry they were seized by the waiting mob and carried onto the street. The head of the Communist column moved off. Others followed as quickly as the placards could be painted.

In the middle of the confusion a runner appeared at the door of Communist Headquarters. Ever since a Korean had won a cross-country race for the Japanese in one of the Olympic games, the Koreans had adopted cross-country running as the national sport—even the Communists. So no one paid much attention as the sweaty, breathless runner struggled through the crowd and upstairs to the Committee Room. He pulled a moist sweat-covered envelope from under his shirt, passed it to the Chairman, and collapsed in a corner. The Chairman tore it open, read it through hurriedly and clapped his hand to his head.

"My God," he murmured, "we're for it—for trusteeship."

He hurried downstairs to where the painters were scribbling away and passed them the word. Another set of slogans was produced and the painters started applying them to the remainder of the stock of blank placards. The Chairman hustled out to the crowded courtyard, climbed on a chair, called for silence and announced:

"Comrades, it has been decided we want trusteeship. The slogan you will shout is, therefore: 'Down with American Imperialism! Hurrah for the Soviet Union! We want a Russo-American trusteeship!' "

Not until that evening when a few ex-Party members, unable to stomach the decision, jumped the traces, did we learn the full delightful tale of what had gone on at C.P.

Headquarters that morning. Needless to say, Radio Pyong-yang only mentioned the tail of the column.

Early in May the Russian Delegation turned up. The head of the Delegation was a short, fat, round-faced little general named T. Shtikov. At a press conference following his arrival, a Korean journalist asked him what the "T." stood for. "It's a military secret," Shtikov answered solemnly. We never did find out what his first name was. His political deputy was Tsarapkin, a Foreign Office official, at present Malik's deputy in the United Nations, at that time sporting the gilded uni-form of a lieutenant general. The rest of the Delegation in-cluded an Armenian economic expert, and a couple of colo-nels.

General Hodge gave a dinner for the two delegations at his quarters. It was a straight Hodgian austerity affair. There was one cocktail per guest before dinner and before each plate at the table was one small glass of wine. When Hodge had proposed a toast to the success of the negotiations and we'd knocked back the wine, that was all. No more toasts, no more speeches, no more hands across the caviar.

After dinner, Hodge produced a local magician who pro-ceeded to pull rabbits out of Shtikov's pockets and baby duck-lings out of Tsarapkin's black, curly hair. The Russians be-gan to wonder what the devil they'd got themselves in for. I decided Hodge was little short of a genius.

By ten o'clock the party was over and the Russians went home slightly perplexed. The hearty false camaraderie of the European Front they'd obviously expected was conspicuous by its absence. We were here for business. As the last of the Russians walked out the door, Hodge grinned, nodded to us and darted up to bed. It was already half an hour after his normal bedtime.

The negotiations next day started normally enough with a long wrangle over the agenda. This was settled after a few

days and the Commission broke up into committees. Tsarapkin and I constituted the "Political Committee."

The committee room was one of the ballrooms of an ancient Korean palace. A long green baize table stretched the
length of it. At the appointed hour for our first meeting I
strolled in alone and sat down at the middle of one side of
the table. A moment later Tsarapkin appeared flanked by
about ten other Russians.

"Who are all your pals?" I asked.

"Interpreters and assistants," Tsarapkin explained curtly.

"Well, I'd just as soon talk Russian if it's all right with
you so we can dispense with interpreters and save a little
time," I suggested.

Tsarapkin readily agreed to our speaking Russian and we
started work. The first problem was: How were we going to
select the Korean democratic and social elements with whom
we were going to consult as directed by the Foreign Ministers? We discussed the problem till noon and then broke up
for lunch.

I hurried over to report to General Hodge. I told him about
Tsarapkin's staff. Hodge laughed. "We'll fix that. Leave it
to me."

When three o'clock came I found twenty officers waiting
in my office. "General Hodge's orders to report for conference duty," they said. I waited a few minutes to give Tsarapkin time to get into the conference room. Then followed
by the twenty officers I marched in and sat down. The officers
took chairs beside me, folded their arms and looked straight
ahead of them.

"Who are these?" said Tsrarapkin, startled by the crowd of
glaring officers.

"Oh, just some assistants," I answered casually.

From then on Tsarapkin and I met with one or possibly
two "assistants" each.

Tsarapkin was a somewhat humorless character but he knew all the tricks and used them. After a good deal of argument he and I agreed to exchange lists simultaneously of the Korean Parties each of us proposed should be consulted. Tsarapkin would list the northern parties, and I the southern parties. Thereafter each of us would defend his list with a brief description of the strength, political character and qualities of the parties proposed. I attached considerable importance to the fact that the lists be exchanged simultaneously. If Tsarapkin knew how many and what kind of parties I was proposing he could easily wire back to Pyongyang to organize as many fictitious associations as might be necessary to match or outbid me. Unfortunately in Southern Korea we didn't have that much control over the situation. Because of our difficulties, I was a bit slow in preparing my lists and Shtikov began to complain that Thayer was sabotaging the Conference. But at last I got together a list we thought we could rely on and I came triumphantly to the committee room prepared for the "simultaneous" exchange.

"Well, at long last, have you your list?" Tsarapkin asked.

"Yes, it's right here. Have you got yours?"

"Mine! Why it's been ready here for ten days," he said and patted his briefcase.

I tossed my list across the table nonchalantly.

"Let's see yours," I said as he picked it up and hastily scanned the eight or ten parties listed. Then he looked up.

"Oh, mine? I didn't bring it along today. I didn't think you'd be ready, you've delayed so long."

"But you just said it was in your briefcase."

"No, I didn't. I just patted my briefcase."

I was furious. Without a word I got up, slammed my briefcase shut, and left the room.

"Don't be angry, Karl Georgevitch," Tsarapkin called soothingly. "It's all good clean sport."

I went to General Hodge and told him what had happened.

"I've been sent out here as a Russian expert supposedly because I know their tricks and then I let them go and pull that on me. Expert, hell!" I stammered with rage.

Hodge and Arnold laughed. "Don't take yourself so damn seriously. You'll get a chance to get even with them."

Our chance came a few days later. I'd just finished describing all the parties I'd suggested be consulted.

Tsarapkin hemmed and hawed and said he understood there was another very powerful party in South Korea not on my list, namely the South Korean Communist Party. It was a question we'd all been waiting for.

"I'm certainly glad you mentioned that," I began to recite. "We'd be delighted to tell you why we didn't include it. Lieutenant Bertsch, here, has made a special study of that organization and I'll just ask him to answer your question."

"The so-called Communist Party of South Korea," Bertsch began, "is a very well-organized, well-disciplined, well-financed group (though I'll be damned if I know where they get their money). They claim to be very progressive. They've got a very plausible program and some excellent slogans which they are very clever at popularizing."

"Then why don't we consult it?" said Tsarapkin somewhat puzzled at all the apparent praise Bertsch was heaping on the Communists.

"Well, the only trouble with it is, it isn't a political party at all. Our purpose in consulting with Korean parties is, I think, to find out what the parties, what their members, what the mass of Koreans in general think and what they want. Isn't that so?"

"Yes," mumbled Tsarapkin, not quite sure what was coming next.

"Well, the so-called South Korean Communist Party isn't that kind of a party at all."

"What is it then?" asked Tsarapkin belligerently.

"Of course, I don't know too much about it, but I do know that it represents some non-Korean outfit. It never asks its members what they want. It merely tells them what it has been told by its bosses is good for them. No South Korean Communist Party member has the slightest say in what the Party does. It goes through a sort of ritual of congresses and conferences but invariably the decisions come from above."

"Just what are you implying, Lt. Bertsch?" Tsarapkin shouted angrily, wondering no doubt how all this was going to look on the record when it was published.

"Don't get excited," I broke in soothingly. "You asked us to tell you about it and we're telling you." I whispered loudly to my stenographer to take down all Bertsch had said, in full, for the minutes.

"But where do all these orders from above you're talking about originate?"

"I'm glad you asked that question," Bertsch replied. "It's a very good question. To tell you the truth, we really can't give you the answer definitely. I've no documentary proof of where the ultimate origin is. We know, of course, that the money comes from outside Southern Korea and so do all the directives. Take for instance the Anti-Trusteeship Parade. When the Communists' Paraders started from their headquarters they were shouting 'Down with Trusteeship.' Then a little Korean runner arrived from somewhere and suddenly the tail end of the column began shouting 'Hurrah for Trusteeship.' The 'will of the people' as the Communists here call it got changed without the people even knowing about it. They were out on the street shouting when it shifted."

"This is pure sophistry," Tsarapkin barked. "You've no proof. It's Jesuitical. Where did the messenger you talk about come from?"

"That's another good question," Bertsch answered. "When we asked him, he said he came from Northern Korea. He'd run a good deal of the way from the 38th Parallel, he said. But, of course, you can't be sure. He was angry at the Communists because, he said, they didn't pay him enough for the journey. So you see he was prejudiced. Of course, he may have come from China or Japan. Perhaps he swam the China Sea. You can't ever be sure."

Tsarapkin was beside himself.

"I want proof. Have you the slightest proof?"

"No, not of the ultimate source of the directives and the money," Bertsch admitted. "But perhaps you could help out there."

"Proof!" Tsarapkin demanded again.

"We have this much proof," Bertsch went on and tossed a document across the table. "It's a directive to the Central Committee of the South Korean Communist Party on its attitude toward the negotiations we are now carrying on. It's an interesting document and should please you. It very strongly supports your position. In fact it contains a good deal of information about our talks that we've agreed should be confidential."

Tsarapkin glanced at the document and pushed it aside. "Where does it come from?"

"As you see by the seal it comes from an organization that styles itself the Communist Party of Northern Korea. It's signed by Kim-il Sung, the leader of that organization. The document was found on a man who crossed the Parallel illegally last week. He said he received it in Pyongyang and had orders to deliver it to the Communist Party Headquarters here in Seoul. You should read it."

Tsarapkin was about to say something but Bertsch didn't give him a chance to interrupt.

"Of course, I realize that the orders and the money don't originate in Pyongyang. I'm sure they come from somewhere else. That's where I thought you could help. Perhaps you could tell us where the Communist Party of Northern Korea gets its orders?"

This time Tsarapkin got up, slammed his briefcase shut and stalked out of the room.

But our extra-curricular relations with the Soviet Delegation were not always as frigid as over the green baize table. Not long after I'd arrived in Seoul, I met a representative of the American Red Cross, Paul Chavchavadze. Before the Revolution, when Stalin's name was still Djugashvili, the Chavchavadzes had their estates near Stalin's birthplace in Georgia. So when I was introduced I asked, for lack of something better to say:

"An old neighbor and acquaintance of the Djugashvilis, I presume?"

Paul drew himself up with mock dignity.

"Sir," he said with a put-on pompous air, "the Djugashvilis knew the Chavchavadzes but the Chavchavadzes did not know the Djugashvilis." He paused and smiled. "But now it's the other way round."

Paul was most anxious to see what some of his ex-countrymen were like, since he'd left Russia at the time of the Revolution. So one evening I invited one of the more agreeable officers on the Soviet Delegation in for a drink and dinner at the hotel. Lest the officer be scared off by a Russian prince, I told Paul to drop into my room as though by accident after the officer had arrived and then we could see whether he showed signs of panic, in which case Paul could leave.

The officer arrived on schedule and by the time Paul

showed up I'd managed to relax him with a couple of quick Martinis.

I introduced them in Russian.

"Colonel, I'd like to present Mister Paul Chavchavadze who also speaks Russian."

The Colonel, who prided himself on his manners, bowed, stuck out his hand and without a blink answered:

"*Prince* Chavchavadze, I presume, would be more correct?" Paul admitted as much.

"I've heard so much of your aunt, the Grand Duchess, from my mother," the colonel explained. "This is a most pleasant surprise." Any doubts about the meeting evaporated immediately.

The Colonel, who came apparently from a bourgeois family in Petersburg, had been brought up on gossip from the Czar's court. Paul's aunt and various other members of his family had been active in court circles for years before the Revolution.

"Now tell me what ever became of Her Royal Highness the Archduchess Elizabeth?" the Colonel asked as he sipped his Martini delicately. "Living in Paris, you say, and has three children—now isn't that nice? Two girls and a boy. That's splendid. I'll write to my mother tonight and tell her. She'll be so pleased.

"And His Highness the Archduke? Dead? Oh, I'm dreadfully sorry to hear that. I can remember my mother pointing him out when he went riding around Tsarskoe Selo. What a pity he was killed. By the Bolsheviks, you say? Oh my! My mother will be distressed. Those were dreadful times!"

We went down to dinner and they kept right on talking about Prince this and Princess that. After dinner we sat down in the bar. The Colonel was having the time of his life, indulging his hereditary love of royalty to the gills. And Paul, too, was obviously enjoying the intense interest

and curiosity of the official of the classless society in the wel-
fare of the families his regime had sent spinning from their
palaces to the garrets of Western Europe. Thirty years of
proletariatization hadn't knocked the snobbery out of our
colonel. I recalled the young lieutenant who'd arrested me
in Austria and his almost reverent attitude to the Austrian
prince. I remembered the story of the old Austrian archduke
who had received the obsequious homage of the Russian lib-
erating troops, seated on a throne he'd dug out of the attic
of his schloss, for the occasion. And I wondered if the possibility of a new Russian nobility was quite as far-fetched as
it had once seemed. It was nearly three o'clock when I left
Chavchavadze and the Colonel still going strong.

The Soviet strategy for the conference became clear soon
enough. They would consult with, and permit to participate
in, a future Korean Government only those Korean parties
and individuals who were completely subservient ("friendly"
they called it) to the Soviet Union and the Communist
Party. One of the criteria they would use to eliminate
any others was opposition to the trusteeship proposal. This
itself included ninety-five percent of the non-Communists.
For the other five percent they'd find other criteria to bar
them from public office. The result—if it worked—would be
another satellite. After weeks of tedious negotiation it also
became clear that the Russians were not prepared to compromise. In the meantime the political development of Korea was at a standstill and its economy, split in two, was
rapidly going to pot. The best we could do was not to yield
an inch, but to build our case for public opinion so clearly
and so solidly that when the inevitable break came there
would be no doubt anywhere outside the Soviet orbit that
we'd done our best to wipe out the 38th Parallel and reunite
Korea under a democratic regime.

One problem in such situations is the Soviet habit of using all the most respectable political phrases; not only "democracy," but "freedom," "liberty," "popular suffrage" ("will of the people," they called it), ascribing to them concepts entirely different from their accepted meaning. Thus the record of what they said read beautifully but meant exactly the reverse. Our job was to get them to say what they meant in words that meant what the dictionary said they meant. You could scarcely have found a better man for the job than the blunt, direct, patient General Arnold.

Arnold was a most impressive looking fellow to begin with. A big man with a big head, with plenty of room between the ears, a good stock of grey hair, a prominent beaklike nose, he would sit there facing the round pudgy little Shtikov like an eagle watching an overfed chipmunk.

Shtikov had one trait that was unfortunate, for him at least. He used to lose his temper. And when he lost his temper, he'd use the words he really meant, not the pretty code words like democracy, and so forth. One of our more useful approaches was to cite the rights the Soviet Constitution ostensibly granted Soviet citizens. Did Shtikov suggest the Koreans should be permitted only a second class constitution? Shtikov invariably hit the ceiling at that one.

"Of course not," he said time and again, but as his proposals belied his words and as we kept repeating our question, he got angrier and angrier.

"Let's face facts," he said at last. "Constitutions are fine for people who have proved themselves worthy of them. We Soviet citizens waited from 1917 to 1936 before Stalin gave us a democratic constitution. And for the Koreans it must be the same. They must first prove they're worthy of being treated democratically. Only then can we permit them the gift of a democratic constitution."

Arnold turned to the stenographer:

"You got all of that, didn't you?" Then he said to Shtikov, "That's what I thought you meant all along, General. Thank you."

Shtikov looked red and flustered. His more sober colleagues squirmed visibly. But it was in the record.

I used to sit next to Arnold and listen to Shtikov speaking Russian. While the interpreting was going on I scratched a rough draft of a suggested reply. Sometimes Arnold would read it out, or revise it or simply lay it aside. One hot day as Shtikov's temper was rising I was passing note after note to Arnold. Impassively and invariably courteously Arnold put one awkward question after another to Shtikov. Shtikov rose and began to pound the table while his deputies began to pass note after note, too, trying to calm him down. But he brushed them imperiously aside and went on shouting at the imperturbable Arnold. At last Arnold, having glanced at a note from me, looked up.

"The American Delegation has nothing further to add."

"Oh, yes, you do!" shouted Shtikov furiously. "I saw that note they passed you. What does it say?" He was beside himself.

"If you insist, General, the note says, 'I think he's sore enough for today.' Shall we adjourn till tomorrow?"

Shtikov was still spluttering like an angry jaybird when Arnold rose to his full six foot three and stalked solemnly out of the conference room.

After seven long weeks of haggling the record was as clear as we could make it. So we suggested bluntly to the Russians that they agree to implement the Moscow decision to give Korea a democratic government according to the standard meanings of those words or go home. They went home.

With the Russians back north of the 38th Parallel, my assignment in Korea was finished—but not the job. That had only begun.